THE FACULTY
IN HIGHER EDUCATION

THE FACULTY IN
HIGHER EDUCATION

by DEANE G. BORNHEIMER

Chairman, Higher Education Program
NEW YORK UNIVERSITY

GERALD P. BURNS

President
OUR LADY OF THE LAKE COLLEGE, SAN ANTONIO, TEXAS

GLENN S. DUMKE

Chancellor
THE CALIFORNIA STATE UNIVERSITY AND COLLEGES

THE INTERSTATE PRINTERS & PUBLISHERS, INC.
Danville, Illinois

CONTENTS

SECTION TWO—BUILDING THE FACULTY

SECTION THREE—PROBLEMS OF THE FACULTY

PREFACE

Throughout the ages, the philosophers have told us that man's most important characteristic is his ability to think. As he thinks, he learns and his behavior changes. This change in behavior has been, and still is, called education.

Man, the rational animal, can be said to base his educational process on thinking and learning. These activities can be spontaneous and instinctive, but generally they constitute a conscious exercise of the will and intellect.

The ability to think and the capacity to learn exist to some degree in every human being. As functions of the mind, they can be increased or retarded by external stimulation.

The factors that provide such stimulation, and that influence education or growth, can be catalogued under two major headings—informal and formal. In terms of environment, the home is an example of an informal situation wherein education occurs; the school and the college are examples of places wherein formal education occurs.

In terms of people, to extend the simple illustration above, the family contributes to the informal education of the children; the teachers and professors contribute to the formal education of children, youth, and adults.

Of course, the opportunity is present for teaching and learning, both formal and informal, to some extent in nearly every environment; and nearly everyone teaches something to somebody at some time. Indeed, the field of education in many ways is as broad as life itself, for in the normal person every conscious moment offers at least some infinitesimal sensation which must exert an influence on the organism.

Narrowing our concern to the field of formal education still presents a universe of considerations. Even limiting our coverage to higher education—to colleges and universities—offers a spectrum of study too immense for this single effort. Thus, we seek to deal merely with one aspect of higher education—the teachers in our colleges and universities, commonly called the faculty.

The sages proclaim that education is the most important activity of man and mankind. There is ample evidence to substantiate the truth of that contention. In fact, it can be documented that the longer man lives on this planet, the more important becomes his education.

As this process of thinking and learning increases in importance to civilization, the methods of activating it likewise increase in importance. Since man learns by thinking and doing, the formal techniques of consciously influencing this activity deserve careful consideration.

Man learns best from other men. If those other men are skilled and dedicated teachers, technically and substantively, the opportunity is present for him to learn qualitatively and quantitatively more than if they are poor teachers. In addition to the human stimulators of thought and action, there are innumerable mechanical teachers of great value. However, at the risk of over-simplifying, it should be understood that the picture, the book, the teaching machine, and even the computer are directly dependent upon the artist, the author, the programmer, and the scientist—all teachers of sorts.

Thus, as we focus on man's need for education, we move from the generalities of instinctive and informal influences on behavior to the particularities of conscious and formal teaching and learning. The stage will be the colleges and universities; the performers will be the instructors and professors; the setting will be a scholarly and academic one.

The most important people in colleges and universities are the faculty members. They are the essential ingredient for several reasons. Theirs is the primary responsibility for conducting the academic program of the institution. And the academic program is the basic reason for having colleges and universities.

In addition to their role in conducting the educational operations of institutions of higher learning, the faculty members are the people in closest and most continuous contact with the students. They are the key people who meet with the students in classes, laboratories, seminars, and other learning situations. They are the core of the college or university that is expected to remain on campus and give continuity over the years to the institution.

It is acknowledged that the functions of colleges and universities are changing. Such changes will, of course, affect the role of the faculty. But, in the main, the responsibility of instructors and professors is to teach. This is especially true in the undergraduate colleges. In the graduate schools of the university, faculty members have broader roles that include, along with teaching, concern for research and in many cases community services. It is emphasized, however, that although there are these differences in the responsibilities of graduate faculty and undergraduate faculty members, the issues discussed and concerns expressed in this book are equally applicable to and appropriate for both groups.

Along with heavy emphasis on teaching, the faculty member in the small college frequently carries on considerable student advising and occasionally tutorial activity. Both of these functions might be classed under teaching, since they deal with students in a specialized learning situation. Thus, in this study of the faculty in higher education, we will be discussing the functions and relationships of teachers in general, realizing that differences exist on various campuses, but that there are common threads running through the fabric of academic activity in all colleges and universities.

Considering the importance of the faculty to the existence of institutions of higher learning, it is interesting that so few definitive studies have been made and books written on this dynamic subject. There are several available on specific aspects of the area, but few that deal with it in terms of its basic problems and three major components as indicated herein. The authors have carefully perused the available literature of the field and commented on pertinent passages from appropriate publications. We have avoided extensive references to the works of others, but have documented materials quoted.

This book is arranged to treat the subject in logical sequence, moving from the general functions of the faculty, through obtaining and organizing the faculty, to the specific problems of the faculty. Within each of these three main divisions are sections or chapters that deal with particular aspects of the faculty's relationship to the students and their institutions.

The book is written in candid fashion. We have avoided the temptation to discuss merely the good things going on in academe. We have taken a position on many of the controversial issues facing higher education today. We have avoided professional jargon and educational clichés, preferring to present our feelings and observations in simple, straight-forward language. Through this approach we hope that this book will find not only readers from the ranks of the educators, scholars, and scientists, but also those who markedly influence educational policy, such as administrators, board members, and foundation officers. Indeed, there may be found herein some food for thought on the part of students, parents, and all of those who would seek the best kind of educational programs for our nation.

It is unlikely that any one study or book could cover adequately all considerations related to a subject as broad as this. However, we have tried to focus on those items of greatest relevance to the current problems of higher education in America. It is also unlikely that every reader will agree with all our observations and conclusions. No attempt is made to please everyone; a sincere attempt is made to present factually our viewpoints on the existing situation, how it developed historically, and what the future holds for it.

Our aim is to interpret and inform; to present observations that may favorably affect the future of those who teach and those who study. It is hoped that many who labor in these groves of academe will find the treatment both instructive and inspirational. Undoubtedly it will prove irritating to some, reassuring to others, and perhaps challenging to the remainder.

There are few if any aspects of the field of higher education in which there exist more folk-lore, fantasy, or fallacies than in that pertaining to the faculty. No single study could expose all, or even touch on the majority, of these vagaries. However, at the risk of tilting educational windmills, or even rocking the academic boat, it strikes us that the time is late and the need is great for thoughtful and honest consideration of the pressing problems in this area.

As Professor Drucker reminds us, "Any first attempt at converting folklore into knowledge, and a guessing game into a discipline, is liable to be misread as a downgrading of individual ability and its replacement by a rule book. Any such attempt would be nonsense, of course. No book will ever make a wise man out of a donkey or a genius out of an incompetent. . . ."[1]

It would be incorrect to imply that this volume was the result of our efforts alone. Many of the facts presented and opinions offered herein are based upon suggestions from studies and experiences of others. Although as authors we take full responsibility for all contained in the book, we acknowledge with deep gratitude the enormous value of the assistance rendered by friends, associates, and learned colleagues across the nation. While it is impossible to list by name all those who provided

1. Peter F. Drucker, *Managing for Results,* New York: Harper and Row, 1964, xii.

advice, guidance, and stimulation, it is accurate to observe that this book could not have been written without the aid and inspiration of many of these distinguished scholars, scientists, and educational statesmen.

Finally, we would be remiss if we did not close with a special note of appreciation to Miss Marilou Denbo, Teaching Assistant, New York University, for her assistance in preparing this volume.

Deane G. Bornheimer
Gerald P. Burns
Glenn S. Dumke

New York, New York
July 1973

SECTION ONE

Functions of the Faculty

INTRODUCTION TO SECTION ONE

This first section of the book deals with the basic functions of the faculty in colleges and universities. Subsequent sections will treat of how a faculty is developed and what problems are encountered in maintaining it.

The five major operational areas—teaching, research, service, advisement, and committees—constitute the functional assignments wherein faculty members spend the bulk of their time.

Obviously, by other definitions, there are additional kinds of duties in the groves of academe. But, for purposes of this treatment, described and delimited as the basic *functions, these offer a broad horizon for comment and criticism.*

There is a great temptation to cite specific examples of gifted practitioners in these basic functions. We resist this urge for the following reasons: first, there are readily available excellent publications with such specific illustrations; second, such treatment of detail would expand this book to enormous size; third, particular examples, techniques, even individuals become dated; fourth, we deal with general philosophy, principles, and practices to avoid the overlap, verbosity, and outdatedness mentioned above.

1 TEACHING

It was not until 1966 that the Establishment in higher education decided to take action, and then it was the prestigious American Council on Education that spearheaded the movement. The action, as originally initiated, was to devote ACE's entire annual meeting to the consideration of the plight of teaching in colleges and universities.

There are many weaknesses in higher education, and among the greatest of these is the poor quality of teaching carried on in our higher institutions. And this situation was getting worse, rather than better, when the American Council met and proposed remedial action. The ACE noted that lamenting the deterioration of college teaching and related duties is futile. Rather it is necessary to search for new ways to improve teaching. So said ACE, and so say we in starting such a search in this study.

WHY IS TEACHING DETERIORATING?

The deterioration of teaching can be traced back to the turn of the century. There were several causes for this deplorable situation. Chief among the causes were: (1) the emphasis on research, (2) the autonomy of academic departments, (3) the loyalty to a discipline, (4) faculty control of the curriculum, and (5) the timidity of deans and presidents.

On the first cause, since the discovery of new knowledge is an essential function of educational institutions, research was incorporated early as an important part of a professor's responsibility. In the large universities, especially those tax-supported, this part assumed a disproportionate relationship to all other responsibilities. Research—and its hand-maiden, publication—was richly rewarded, but there was no place in the university reward system for recognition of good teaching. Promotion, tenure, and salary increases went to those whose educational contribution was most measurable and dramatic—namely the research oriented professors. "Many university scientists openly scorn teaching and use their appointment to boil the pot of individual research. Now a life of research is a worthy one, but no amount of worthy motive justifies false pretenses and fraudulent impersonation—in this case the pretense of imparting knowledge and the impersonation of a teacher."[1]

In the last two decades the researchers also found increasing emoluments in grants from foundations, industry, and government. Unhappily, the teaching-oriented professors, who were engaged in the almost unmeasurable, yet vitally important, task of stimulating thinking and transmitting knowledge, received nothing but the disdain and condescension of their colleagues. "The last ten years, beginning with Sputnik, represent a period when the overriding concern of higher education has been with research and graduate education. For the next decade, however, as can be predicted from the evolving policies of Federal agencies, private foundations, and the universities themselves, and as is underlined by the current spasms of student unrest, the primary concern of college educators will be with teaching. Just as the postwar university had to rediscover its mission of 'creating the future' through scholarly and scientific research, so today we must again turn our attention to the primary educational function of the university."[2] This we believe, and we note with satisfaction that the pendulum is really beginning to swing in the direction of increased attention to teaching.

The second reason for the deterioration of teaching can be attributed to departmental neglect. As the curriculum in higher education expanded from the limited concepts of the classics and humanities of the colonial colleges, it was logical that the courses taught should be grouped for purposes of identification, sharing of related knowledge, and administrative purposes. As this grouping into divisions or departments took place along subject-matter lines, the instructors and tutors, the lecturers and professors, began to relate themselves more closely to their departments or divisions than to their college or university. The chief reason for this was that the departments and divisions were virtually autonomous units and the politics of the institution made it desirable to identify with the functioning unit. Within the units, advancement was based upon results in scholarly activities, such as research and publication, rather than upon teaching and advising students. "The basic pattern of undergraduate instruction has not changed at most universities since the turn of the century. At that time the departmental divisions of knowledge were established, a system of credit hours, lectures, and examinations was worked out, and a pattern of 'distribution' and 'concentration' requirements was created. All of these endure to this day. The 'system' was briefly leavened with general education, but this fashion is now being supplanted by independent study. Some institutions have, however, done little to alter the basic style of undergraduate instruction."[3]

The third cause of teaching's being neglected relates to the loyalty of faculty to their discipline, rather than to their institution. They get ahead faster, and it is vastly more interesting, interacting with scholars in their same field instead of with either students or colleagues in the institution concerned with some other discipline. Thus, they are less concerned with teaching students than with producing new knowledge, publishing results, attending scholarly meetings, and consulting with learned societies, industry, and government. Although the philanthropic foundations now deplore this situation, they originally were in the vanguard of agencies encouraging it through the support of scholarly and scientific projects, the funds for which went directly to the researcher rather than through the institution. Sanford agrees with this contention and quotes other experts inclined to this view. "It is a fair surmise that within the profession of college teaching there has been a fairly progressive decline in teaching enthusiasm, as Riesman (1956) has suggested. This is probably especially true in the more advanced, wealthy, and prestigeful institutions that appear at the head of Riesman's 'academic procession.' As Caplow and McGee (1958) point out, the main avenue to employment and promotion for the professor is through scholarly publications and research, and not through demonstrated proficiency in the teaching function."[4]

The fourth reason for the sad plight of teaching is the faculty control exercised over the curriculum. While it is highly desirable for the teachers to have a strong voice in determining what shall be taught at their institutions, theirs should not be the only voice heard. The governing board has an indirect responsibility, and the administration a direct responsibility, in the shaping of the curriculum. Where such responsibilities were abdicated, it was only logical that departmental log-rolling would occur, that course additions or deletions would come about through academic trading, and that more interest would be evinced in teaching fewer hours in a specialized subject than in teaching a heavier load in a general subject. Thus, those junior members who didn't get just what they wanted in terms of course assignments considered most of their teaching a necessary evil. "Today a more commercial spirit is evident in the profession, and it seems to me that one example of it is the way in which we diminish teaching loads. We are a powerful union."[5]

A final cause for poor teaching is the reluctance of deans and presidents to be concerned with the quality and quantity of instruction at their institutions. This is due in part to the myth that faculty members are privileged persons who must be venerated, not coordinated, advised, or administered. But this reluctance to get involved with teaching also stems from the fact that the evaluation of teaching is at best an extremely difficult task and one which the harassed and overworked academic administrator is often satisfied to ignore while more immediate crises occupy his time. Yet, the main purpose for having academic administrators is to assist and advise faculty members in the exercise of their function. Since these administrators have in the past been unwilling or unable to provide the leadership that would help bring about good teaching, it seldom came about.

Thus, as the rich (researchers) get richer, the poor (teachers) get poorer. It is no wonder that the public is beginning to ask about the absentee professors that travel about the world consulting, or disappear into their laboratories never to see a student. It is no wonder that our students feel cheated when some of the most brilliant professors are denied them, when their classes resemble a theatre audience, and when they are instructed by bored or harassed teaching assistants.

Since this problem has been admitted and defined, steps have been proposed for its solution. These will be discussed in the sections that follow.

WHAT IS TEACHING?

Teaching is enabling learning. While some self-teaching can occur, we shall herein deal with teaching as it is directed to others. As a process that attempts to bring about learning, teaching is composed of two major facets—the transmission of knowledge and the stimulation of thinking.

The first facet of teaching is the transmission of knowledge. Traditionally the wisdom of the ages has been passed along to the young by the teachers, scribes, rabbis, and medicine men of the tribes. This transmission of knowledge is not limited to the teachers and professors or the schools and colleges. However, it is through these people and in these environments that it usually takes place.

It is imperative that we be taught, encouraged, and inspired to think. It is not enough to be spoon-fed facts, ideas, and other forms of knowledge. We must learn how to think, reason, and ponder these acquisitions. Our world today has accumulated so much knowledge that no human brain can encompass even a small fraction of the total. Thus, we must be taught to think about and use intellectually that minute portion that we can assimilate. Our world tomorrow will have so much *new* knowledge, that no human brain will be able to assimilate even a small fraction of it. Thus, we must be taught to reason and use the intellectual tools that will permit us to live with and profit from these vast and constantly expanding frontiers of knowledge.

"It is true that like all gifts of nature the ability to think cannot be imparted; it can only be developed, and one of the oldest complaints against schools is that they stop the natural thinker and try to make him a learned dunce. It is only fair to add that determined thinkers are few. For most people, thinking is dreary uphill work; their mind is set in motion by only a rare stimulus. Thinking means shuffling, relating, selecting the contents of one's mind so as to assimilate novelty, digest it, and create order."[6]

For purposes of emphasis and analysis we have separated those two facets of teaching—the stimulation of thinking and the transmission of knowledge. However, this is an artificial separation. The gifted professor will strive to integrate these two objectives in his everyday teaching.

In the elementary and secondary schools, it is essential that the fundamentals or elements of certain basic subjects be taught and learned. With the radical and rapid changes taking place in all disciplines, especially the sciences, it is imperative that more than facts be taught. Of course, even at this level of higher learning, students will need conventional presentations of factual material, especially in the humanities. But a sustained effort is needed to provide the intellectual tools, such as principles, that will not run the risk of becoming obsolete.

HOW DID IT START?

Teaching started the day you were born, and you were your first teacher. If you were cold, you quickly taught yourself to cuddle close to your mother. If you were hungry, you learned that the right cry or word might produce your mother's breast. This was self-teaching and still goes on.

As you grew older your parents taught you how to behave in the home, with the family, and later, what to do and say in and with the public. This was informal teaching and education.

Finally the day came when you went off to school. There you had a trained teacher in an educational environment. There were probably other children involved, and it was a planned program of formal education.

Of course, there were variations to this self-teaching, informal teaching, and formal teaching or education. Other persons and other environments undoubtedly played a role. And in other civilizations, if they were sufficiently primitive, the third step of formal teaching may have been omitted.

In any event, teaching started in an effort to change behavior in order to adapt comfortably to existing or future conditions, situations, or environments. Teaching brings about learning or knowing. As we learn or find out, either consciously or unconsciously, we react. When the baby feels hungry, he learns to eat. When the child is frightened, he learns to run. When the adult is threatened, he learns to react in the way he is taught —to fight back, to draw away, to call for help.

WHO DOES TEACHING?

As mentioned earlier, we are all teachers. Much of what we learn is self-taught. Although self-teaching continues throughout life, as we become members of the family and, later, of the community, considerable formal teaching occurs. "Besides Socrates and Jesus, the great teachers of mankind are mankind itself—your parents and mine."[7]

Thus our parents, and others living in the home, are our early teachers. Others among our early and informal teachers are our playmates, relatives, and visitors. In the community, our semiformal teachers are found in our church or Sunday school and our playground or summer camp.

It is not until we reach school age that we come in contact with those trained people who would formally shape our intellect. As pupils in school, we have teachers; as students in college, we have professors. Others among the professionals who educate us at times are special tutors, and teachers of the arts—such as music, drama, and dance.

In addition to all these teachers with whom we interact face-to-face, we are also taught by persons on radio and TV, films and pictures. And, of course, the printed word in books, magazines, and newspapers remains a great source of passive or inanimate teaching throughout life.

HOW ARE TEACHERS PREPARED?

Teachers are prepared in many ways. A certain amount of natural or instinctive teaching ability is present in and manifested by nearly everyone. In terms of early training, we learn something about teaching as we are taught. How frequently we resort to the old cliché, experience is the best teacher. This simply means we are taught by, or learn from, things that happen to us or others throughout our entire lives.

Formal preparation of teachers occurs in teachers' colleges and schools of education. Prior to these institutions, teachers were trained by apprenticeship—by "sitting in" with experienced teachers. Before that, history discloses that the elders of the tribe, and especially the priests or medicine men, assumed responsibility for informally training their successors. Teaching has been essential since the dawn of civilization for passing along to the young the wisdom and traditions, the taboos and mores of the tribe.

One of the major problems in higher education today is connected with the preparation of teachers. Teachers in elementary and secondary schools have traditionally been trained as teachers. They are given a broad general education, some special instruction in one or more disciplines, and considerable exposure to courses in pedagogy. This kind and extent of general and professional education has served them, their pupils, and our nation faithfully and well. It has given the United States an adequate, if not exceptional, group of dedicated and able school teachers.

However, it was decided early that the most appropriate preparation for those planning careers in college teaching was the research-oriented Ph.D. degree. It was assumed that what little information prospective college teachers needed about teaching could be picked up from their own teachers and professors in the disciplines. Thus, our would-be college professors (with the notable exception of those serving as professors of education) have generally had excellent training in their disciplines and know how to conduct research in their fields, but have received little or no training in the techniques of imparting that subject matter or in the methods of stimulating thinking. "Among other things, I learned in graduate school that teaching is not the most rewarded skill in the academic community. It is perfectly possible to go through a Ph.D. program with every intention of taking a college teaching position upon graduation but without ever having faced a class."[8] So said James R. Hudson, and his experience is not unusual.

WHO IS TAUGHT?

If we consider this question generally, everyone receives some teaching at some time. But, since we are limiting our observations to formal education, we say that in most parts of the world, children go to school at an early age. There they are taught the fundamentals of language and numbers.

Since its founding, our nation has placed enormous importance on education. It is now compulsory in most states for youth to remain in formal education through the high school. In parts of the country it is expected that the majority of our youth will remain in formal education through college.

Prior to the twentieth century, only a small percentage of the population graduated from college. College attendance was considered a privilege reserved primarily for the sons and daughters of families of means. Now, however, college attendance is not reserved for the privileged few, but it is considered as a right to be enjoyed by every person in our society who has demonstrated an interest in higher education and has the qualifications for admission to some type of higher education institution. Although college costs to students have increased enormously since 1900, the funds available for scholarships in private institutions and the virtually free tuition in public institutions has made higher education available today to individuals from all segments of society.

Two of the most current answers to the question, "Who is taught?" are: (1) many of those socio-economic groups previously denied an adequate education, and (2) many of those previously considered too old for formal higher education. On the first point, minority groups, such as Negroes, Puerto Ricans, and American Indians, who in the past received poor education at the lower levels, are being provided with special teaching and training designed to enable them to narrow the educational and cultural gap, and to gain admission and succeed in college. On the second point, formal higher education for adults, and even for senior citizens, is making great strides in enriching the lives and providing collegiate level training for persons previously considered beyond college age.

Private support from foundations and corporations has been followed by public support for offering special teaching and learning opportunities for the economically and educationally disadvantaged, especially in the urban areas. One of the most significant of these developments is the open admissions program of The City University of New York.

The same mixture of support is making possible school and college-level education for adults. The State University of New York has shown leadership in this field with the establishment of the Empire State College, a non-residential college offering courses and programs leading to the Bachelor of Arts and

Associate in Arts degrees. The college, which consists of a network of centers and divisions, works closely with public and private colleges in New York State to serve students of all ages who cannot attend regular classes on traditional campuses because of time restrictions or career obligations.

WHERE DOES TEACHING OCCUR?

As indicated above, the home was probably the first teaching and learning environment for all of us. This was followed by teaching occurring in the yard or garden, and eventually in community areas such as the playground and the church.

Formal teaching and education begin in the nursery school, kindergarten, or first grade of school. These are the environments of education to which the inquiring mind of the child is first exposed. In most instances, the child starts out in a modified classroom, continues through many of them in the various higher grades, and spends most of his college days confined to them.

Research on educational environments has proven that considerable teaching and learning of great value occur outside the classroom and laboratory. The athletic fields, the dormitories, the commons, and other places where students interact with their peers as well as with teachers have proven to be environments conducive to intellectual, physical, and emotional growth.

WHAT ARE THE REWARDS TO TEACHERS?

The greatest reward to any teacher is to witness the intellectual growth he has brought about in another human being. This, of course, is an intangible reward, but it is one of the ennobling gifts in life that make all else worthwhile.

Among the tangible rewards to teachers and professors are salary, security, stimulation, prestige, and service and research opportunities. While educators' salaries have only lately begun to approach those of other professions, the security of a teaching career is usually an element that, because of annual contract or indefinite tenure, has proven attractive. The stimulation of working with children and youth, and of developing their mental abilities, offers intangible rewards to many. The prestige of being a school teacher or college professor, and thus being considered a learned man, provides a sense of satisfaction for many in the educational fraternity. The prospect of serving society in one of its most important functions is a factor that influences teachers to stay in this profession. And, finally, the opportunity for research and writing, for the discovery of and reporting on new knowledge, is a compelling reason for people to embrace academe.

As implied earlier, it is logical to assume that some research will be conducted by nearly every academician. Indeed, there are few teachers who would wish to play an important role in *disseminating* knowledge without playing some role in *developing* knowledge. The problem as we see it is that in recent years the rewards for teaching have been less intriguing than those for research. Some say that the interest of the federal government has been the primary reason for this. President Horn observed that, "The nature of federal support of research is in danger of destroying the whole process of higher education. Some faculty members show an aversion to the undergraduate student. The most prestigious professor of all is the one who has no students at all."[9]

Unquestionably there exists a need for more and better research and experimentation in education. This is particularly true in teaching, and especially at the higher levels. Not only is there a need for such activity, but once accomplished, proven, and accepted, it should be implemented on a broad basis. Nowhere does a wider gap exist between research and application than in the field of teaching and learning. As Professor Woodring has wisely observed, "It is now clear that, as a nation, we have entered into a period of dramatic educational reform that will bring substantial changes to all levels of education, from the nursery school through the university. And, in a time of change, it is essential that programs of teacher education prepare teachers for the schools of the future rather than those of the past."[10]

But the philanthropic foundations with their research projects and the giant corporations with their contract research must share responsibility for this former de-emphasis of teaching in favor of research.

WHAT IS ACADEMIC FREEDOM?

The legal definition of academic freedom appears to be determined by the side on which one wishes to argue. Most generally accepted is the *idea* of academic freedom—that a teacher or professor is free to teach or profess, without interference, any and all aspects of that course or subject in which he is professionally qualified. In addition, it is expected that a faculty member will have all of the rights and the responsibilities of any other citizen to express himself off campus on any and all subjects without reference to his position or profession. However, it goes without saying that society expects persons of prominence in the professions to exercise restraint in terms of decorum and delivery in making public pronouncements.

This briefly enunciated concept of academic freedom is, of course, based upon that propounded by President A. Lawrence Lowell in his defense of Professor Harold Laski's teaching at Harvard, and is generally accepted by board members, administrative offices, and faculty members alike.

WHAT TEACHING AIDS ARE AVAILABLE?

Research in education, especially in this area of the psychology of learning and the communication of ideas, in the last several years has provided an unusual array of helpful aids for the teacher. While his greatest tool remains the book, or the printed word in some other form, he now has innumerable devices to expand and improve the quality of his teaching.

These aids vary from such tried and true equipment as the chalk board and the older audio-visual materials, to the jet-age hardware of the electronic computer and closed circuit color television. Even newer and more exciting innovations are in the experimental stages, with such devices as will place the full resources of general or specialized libraries and museums at the instant disposal of students and teachers. These hookups for information retrieval on a group or individual basis will be available by simply dialing an appropriate number, pressing the right button, or flipping the correct switch.

There is a complete literature which deals factually with these startling innovations and a number of new books that speculate on the miracles in store for teachers and learners in the decade ahead. One cannot help forming the opinion that while education has made modest progress in incorporating new techniques of research and experimentation developed in the last several years, those now emerging seem little short of miraculous in contrast. One other conclusion follows from a study and evaluation of past, present, and future devices for improving instruction —it is that all of these revolutionary aids will enormously *supplement* but never *supplant* the teacher. Regardless of the incredible speed of the computer or the impeccable logic of a teaching machine, nothing as yet envisioned in even the most fertile mind can out-weigh the essential value of the gifted teacher appearing in person.

WHAT RESEARCH OCCURS ON TEACHING?

As indicated above, a host of distinguished scholars, scientists, and skilled technicians have dedicated themselves to developing ways and means, in soft-ware and hard-ware, for the improvement of teaching and, thus, the enrichment of learning. This research embraces all aspects of the field of education, and gratifying results are occurring in many areas.

In terms of pedagogy, or the act of teaching, subject-matter specialists are teaming up with communications experts to bring about a metamorphosis in teaching such diverse courses as the new mathematics on the one hand and social sciences on the other. And some leaders in higher education now realize that a college instructor can no longer be expected to perform adequately merely because he holds a Ph.D. in his subject from a distinguished university. By the same token, it is understood that heavy exposure to methods courses in a teachers college or school of education, without adequate study of one or more subject-matter areas, does not qualify a graduate to teach in the disciplines.

Although research provided valid conclusions on this issue some years ago, it has been only recently that general agreement was reached that training in both pedagogy and education in the subject-matter was imperative for success in teaching at the higher levels. The emphasis on scholarship to the virtual exclusion of the scientific skills of teaching has caused many of our finest colleges and universities to offer less than the best programs for preparing effective college and university teachers.

As documented at the 1966 annual meeting of the American Council on Education (mentioned earlier), research, experimentation, and evaluation further disclose that teaching in higher education, at both undergraduate and graduate levels, needs and deserves to be upgraded and improved. Since the primary job of the college (and even the university) is to teach students, greater effort is needed to attract and retain gifted and dedicated teachers, rather than research scholars and expert consultants in various public services.[11]

HOW IS TEACHING EVALUATED?

The persons who know the most about instruction are, obviously, teachers. Assuming they can be impartial and objective, they are the professional group that should evaluate the teaching offered at their (and other) institutions. This should not preclude deans and other academic administrators from rendering judgments on performance and production, because in most instances these people were faculty members for extended periods. Indeed, it seems ridiculous that the fallacy still exists that the administrators of an institution (department chairmen, academic deans, and presidents) should be denied the right of visiting classrooms and laboratories in their own institutions. These academic administrators should be charged with the responsibility for such visitation in order to advise and assist faculty members to achieve greater teaching ability. And ideally faculty members will welcome such visits, hopefully having become accustomed to them as a result of teaching under supervision during the doctoral training program. Thus, evaluations might be made more effectively, the gifted teacher rewarded, and the inept teacher helped professionally. Obviously, good teachers would welcome such visits, and poor teachers would fear such visits, and the learners would profit either way.

In addition to peer judgments about teaching ability and the resultant learning, whether by fellow faculty members or administrators, evaluations should be made by the group that is exposed most directly and continuously to the process—the students. A few outstanding institutions have encouraged faculty evaluations by students, and some (such as Reed College and Princeton University) have achieved unusual results thereby.

Since teaching is an activity heavily dependent upon the personalities of the instructor and the student(s), it is frequently said to be more of an art than a science. Undoubtedly there is some validity to this assertion. But science, through empirical research and careful evaluation, has proven that with careful training the ability to teach can be markedly improved. Therefore, to the extent that the physician, the lawyer, and other professional practitioners are artists, so too is the college professor. However, since the inculcation of the scientific principles of pedagogy can immeasurably enhance the caliber of instruction, it is our feeling that teaching is more of a science (to be learned) than an art (to be inherited).

WHAT IS LEARNER MOTIVATION?

Motivation is that subtle something which produces desire. The great teacher is the one who causes his pupils to desire to learn. This kind of desire, or learner motivation, is brought about through the skillful application of the scientific principles mentioned above. Without some degree of motivation in the student, it is unlikely that learning can or will take place. Thus it is that the embryonic pedagogue will give serious consideration to those areas of educational and personal psychology that deal with individual and group motivation.

To say that the appropriate desire to learn can be induced entirely through the application of scientific principles would be a mistake. Certainly the "art of teaching," the ability to influence instinctively, and the quality of leadership which unconsciously affects those it touches—all of these methods can have the desired motivational effect.

In these days of artificial stimuli and constant assault on the senses, the effective faculty member will utilize a wide range of motivational factors beyond himself and the institution's resources. Reference is made to the bombardment of the eye and ear through the mass media, much of which is commercial and useless, but some of which is educational and valuable. While we may deplore much of the inane excursions of the Madison Avenue peddlers, some of their methods in motivation are worth studying, and a few can be applied to teaching.

HOW DOES TEACHING VARY IN DIFFERENT INSTITUTIONS?

There are those who feel that teaching is the same, regardless of the environment; we are not among those. The variations between methods of teaching in an informal setting such as the home and those used in a formal setting such as the classroom are great and are numerous. For example, such instruction as given children by parents is usually brief, verbal, and directly related to an immediate issue. Alternatively, instruction as given students by a professor is usually extensive, more than verbal (using books, charts, diagrams, experiments, and other visual aids), and is related to a non-immediate issue.

However, the variations between techniques and quality of teaching in different kinds of higher institutions are equally as great, but much more subtle. The differences that occur are frequently due to the kind of persons teaching and the subject-matter being taught, rather than the institutions *per se*. For example, in the teacher training institutions and the state colleges, the subject matter usually is technical and the instruction is adequate. In the liberal arts colleges, usually the subject matter is covered in scholarly fashion and the teaching is more than adequate. In the great universities, frequently the subject matter is covered adequately, but because much of the instruction is provided by teaching assistants, without any direction or assistance from the professor in charge, the methods of presentation often leave much to be desired.

This is not to say that the small institutions always provide better instruction. Occasionally in the great universities a gifted teacher will prefer the classroom to the laboratory, and will make a profound contribution to his students. However, experience has proven that these men are the exception rather than the rule.

WHAT ARE CONDITIONS FOR GOOD TEACHING?

There are several special factors affecting teaching that should be mentioned, if only briefly at this point. These factors are workload, sabbaticals, tenure, facilities, and professional commitment. The first four involve considerations given the faculty member and the final item involves what he gives to higher education generally and his institution specifically.

The *workload* of faculty members deserves more lengthy consideration than this short paragraph. But, the principle to be enunciated at this point can be summarized as follows. There is no rule of thumb that can be applied precisely to determine the exact number of hours a faculty member should put in at his classroom, laboratory, or office. Suffice to recognize that there are educational responsibilities that must be accepted by teachers, researchers, and other professional employees. These involve commitments or assignments that vary from six classroom hours to twenty per week. Within this variation occurs research, office, laboratory, committee, and other official time allocations. Obviously, if a faculty member has too great a workload, problems will ensue in his performance; alternatively, if he is not pulling his weight in the boat, problems will ensue with his colleagues.

Sabbaticals, those special periods of off-campus activity occurring (theoretically) every seven years, are unique to higher education. Because of the nature and scope of teaching and research, faculty members need and deserve these extended vacations. Actually, the year with half pay or half year with full pay, away from the regular program of the institution, is not always a vacation, but at least it should be a change of pace. Frequently, this time is spent in travel, special study, writing, or just plain recreation. It defeats its purpose—to refresh, enrich, and relax the individual—if it is spent on another similar educational assignment.

Tenure is insurance—insurance that the faculty member will not be arbitrarily terminated without careful consideration. It is contractual protection for the faculty member who has proven himself for a reasonable period, usually three to five years. Because some teaching occasionally engenders the displeasure of some trustees, donors, administrators, politicians, or articulate citizens, faculty members, especially teachers, need and deserve this element of protection and security.

Facilities for teaching. The approach a college professor takes toward teaching a particular class is often not determined by the educational needs of his students and the goals of the course, but rather is determined for him by factors over which he has no control. Among these factors are the facilities for teaching available to him. These facilities include space, equipment, and supplies. Since the emphasis of the institution (liberal arts, professional, or graduate education), plus the size and flexibility of the budget, has a direct bearing on the available facilities, they will vary in every institution. The principle here is that while the faculty member (the person) is the most important factor in the teaching process, the facilities (space, lighting, furniture, and teaching aids) available to him are almost as important and deserve greater consideration in planning than they have had in the past.

The *professional commitment* of faculty members is, in general, not unlike that of men in other professions, such as law, medicine, and the ministry. A professional man must be concerned with ethical values, social concomitants, and the development of the field and its practitioners. Specifically, the faculty member has additional commitments which transcend those of the usual professional man. Reference is made to such responsibilities as cover the entire spectrum of scholarly reflection and educational action. At one end sits the poet and philosopher, Thoreau, by Walden; and, at the other paces the Commissioner of Education in Washington. The professional commitments of the educator are exemplified in each and suggested again in the old saying that he should act like a man of thought, and think like a man of action.

HOW CAN THINKING BE STIMULATED?

The motivation of thinking is one of the current concepts receiving renewed consideration in higher education. Gifted teachers throughout history have taught the techniques of rational thought as part of their general procedures. But, in the past century, education became more concerned with the pragmatic approach of teaching subject matter without too much regard for the intellectual exercise of analysis, speculation, and synthesis that should accompany it. Methods of logical reasoning, careful evaluation, and rational judgment can and should be taught in concert with every academic discipline. One of the best ways to accomplish this objective of motivating learning and encouraging critical thinking is to arouse the curiosity of the student.

Knowledge of specific and sometimes unrelated facts is no longer a valid objective of higher education. It has been replaced by the desire to develop in the student a greater integration of knowledge, increased purposefulness in application, and more intensive desire for further study. Principles must be taught—not bare facts. Man's body of knowledge is now so huge, is expanding with such rapidity, and is so relative (changeable) that factual information taught today may be irrelevant or even out-dated tomorrow.

Team teaching has been tried and proven valuable in elementary and secondary education. This method of pooling the resources of two or more teachers in the same cooperative effort is in the experimental stages in higher education. Because of the increasing complexity of the subject matter being presented in colleges and universities, there is every expectation that this concept of teaching will receive wide acceptance.

Another promising trend in teaching is that of combining several different methods of presentation. The lecture method—one teacher up in front, speaking to one class, usually for one hour—held sway in higher education for more than a century. Now, however, we are witnessing the incorporation of several devices in communicating with students. Indeed, some of these are even encouraging the students to communicate with the instructors. Professor Berlyne has observed that "since discussion (classes) offers the opportunity for a good deal of student activity and feedback, it could be (according to theory) and is (according to research results) more effective than typical lectures in developing concepts and problem solving skills."[12]

In addition to the combining of lecture, discussion, and seminar methods of conducting classes, there is a burgeoning interest in using a wide range of audio-video instruments. Programmed teaching machines, varying from the simple question-and-answer

box to the highly sophisticated computerized information retrieval devices, are also being successfully used.

Although they are not really new concepts of learning or
teaching, the current emphasis on collateral reading, and that
on independent study, deserves mention. The flood of paperback
books has brought about a rebirth of interest in reading assignments. The programmed text book is especially effective in many
subject fields. It presents learning in small bites or steps in the
manner of the carefully calculated sequences of the teaching
machine. Related or linked to these teaching and testing machines, these books have proven to be excellent adjuncts to the
conventional instruction.

Independent study is an improved extension of the project
method so popular a generation ago. In fact, many colleges today
are making major calendar revisions to provide a period for such
study. Here again, understanding of particular facts is not the
primary aim—rather, the inculcation of habits of thinking, reasoning, and rationalization are sought. And the notion that students can receive valuable concomitants of education *outside* of
the classroom and laboratory, and from other than the faculty,
is now a proven fact. Travel abroad programs are just one example demonstrating that programs of this type can be both
academically profitable and pleasant experiences. The impulse
to inform, to instruct, to mold, to indoctrinate is as old as the
human race and is universal; thus while studying independently
on campus, at home, or even in public places, the student is
bombarded with many kinds of helpful information, some of
which he might never receive in his formal learning environment.

WHAT ARE THE NEWEST CONCEPTS?

Among the newest concepts of teaching are: (1) that teachers must have better exposure to both their subject matter and

the techniques of teaching it; (2) that teachers must learn how to motivate students to think, both in and out of the classroom; (3) that teachers must de-emphasize the teaching of factual information in favor of emphasizing the teaching of basic and advanced principles within their subject-matter fields; (4) that teachers can and should operate in groups where the subject matter warrants such team teaching; (5) that in-person teaching should be combined with live television and programmed teaching; and (6) that teachers must seek learning outcomes in behavioral terms.

It is absurd to believe that merely because a scholar thoroughly comprehends his discipline he can communicate it expertly to his students. It is equally absurd to believe that merely because a pedagogue thoroughly comprehends the methods and techniques of teaching he can present a discipline, such as history, mathematics, or a language adequately to his students. Professor Skinner and his colleagues at Harvard have conclusively proven that teachers in colleges and universities need and deserve more and better education in both their subject matter or discipline and in their techniques of teaching. Berlyne says, "When one looks at current learning theory, the gap between it and current educational practice appears tremendous, but the gap is narrowing. One should expect to find a variety of teaching methods used in colleges and that teachers should develop a repertoire of skills."[13]

WHAT IS THE FUTURE OF TEACHING?

There is evidence to suggest that some college and university trustees, high ranking administrators, and in some instances even faculty members are aware of and concerned about the poor quality of instruction in their institutions. During the past few years much of this awareness and concern has been intensified as a result of direct pressure from student groups. We predict that the next decade will see students continuing their demand for better teaching, and well they should.

However, if teaching is to be truly recognized as the most important function professors perform, colleges and universities will have to change their reward system so that teaching is recognized as being as important as research and publishing are now. Thus, while the rewards of teaching, both tangible and intangible, are beginning to increase—and indeed there is reason to be optimistic about the future of college teaching—significant gains cannot be made until colleges decide that they really want good teaching and then hire, promote, and financially reward professors good at it.

DOCUMENTATION AND COMMENTARY

1. Jacques Barzun, *Teachers in America,* Garden City, New York: Doubleday Anchor Books, 1954, 86.

2. *The Educational Record,* "Teachers and Teaching," Annual Meeting Issue, Summer, 1966, 47:3,289.

3. Christopher Jencks, "An Anti-Academic Proposal," *The Educational Record,* "Teachers and Teaching," Annual Meeting Issue, Summer, 1966, 47: 3,321.

4. Nevitt Sanford, *The American College,* New York: John Wiley & Sons, Inc., 1962, 298.

5. Dexter Perkins, background paper delivered to the American Council on Education, 49th Annual Meeting.

6. Barzun, 34-35.

7. *Ibid.,* 10.

8. *The Educational Record,* "Teachers and Teaching," 412.

9. Francis Horn, *U.S. News and World Report,* November 21, 1966, 133.

10. Paul Woodring in Robert H. Anderson, *Teaching in a World of Change,* New York: Harcourt, Brace & World, 1966, v.

11. William Arrowsmith, "The Future of Teaching," keynote address delivered to the American Council on Education, Annual Meeting, October 13, 1966.

12. D. E. Berlyne, *Conflict, Arousal, and Curiosity,* New York: McGraw-Hill Book Company, 1960, 60.

13. *Ibid.,* 7.

2 RESEARCH

Research is the function or activity of seeking the truth. As the word indicates, a search is involved. The search is made to uncover new knowledge or to verify existing factual information. While the function is directed by the intellect, it frequently includes physical activity of major dimensions.

Most research conducted on college or university campuses falls into two categories, pure and applied. Pure research is that conducted without concern for its immediate practical use; it is sometimes called "theoretical." Other research is that conducted for a practical purpose; it is usually called "applied."

WHO DOES RESEARCH?

Members of the teaching faculty of higher education institutions are the people who carry on most of the research programs on campus. Some institutions employ persons specifically as researchers; but in the main, the persons hired as teachers are the research scientists and scholars.

It is precisely on this point—teaching and research—that one of the major problems in higher education is centered. The primary purpose of or for colleges and universities is to provide for the education of students. This education, as mentioned in Chapter 1, is based upon the logical notion that the persons providing this education are doing so chiefly by teaching.

Originally teachers undertook research—usually pure research —to supplement and enrich the content of their teaching. However, during the past half century, research has eclipsed teaching to the extent that in many of the larger institutions, persons hired as teachers spend the bulk of their working hours as researchers.[1]

WHY DO RESEARCH?

Research is a necessary and desirable function in higher education. It is generally accepted as one of the three basic activities of universities, along with teaching and public service. Since education is concerned with the discovery of as well as the transmission of knowledge, research plays an important role on campus.

In addition to the inherent necessity for the search for new and verification of existing information, there are several other valid reasons for the conduct of research. Among these are: (1) the intellectual stimulation it affords, (2) the sense of measurable accomplishments it gives, and (3) the considerable emoluments it provides.

On the first point, most scholars and scientists need and deserve occasionally to escape from their students and to satisfy their professional inclinations toward investigation and experimentation. They should have the opportunity to work and study on their own, or with distinguished colleagues as part of their institutional assignment, for both personal and professional satisfaction and stimulation. Indeed, it is as a result of these independent study and research activities that faculty members continue to learn and grow intellectually.

On the second point, research can and usually does produce tangible and measurable results; teaching results are less tangible and are difficult to measure. It is important to everyone to know that desirable results accrue from his efforts; research provides this kind of measurement. Unfortunately, however, it is for the very reason that research activity and the ensuing publications can be easily measured—whereas teaching is difficult to evaluate—that the large majority of colleges and universities base their faculty promotion and financial compensation on research productivity rather than teaching effectiveness. And it is from this over-recognition of research and publishing that the much criticized publish-or-perish practice has developed in higher education.

This, then, leads directly to the final point: research provides more rewards for the faculty member than does teaching. Even outside the university, the conduct of research—and its offspring, publication—can be extremely attractive financially. Then too, the prestige value of achieving prominence as a researcher, consultant, or author, is considerable.

WHERE IS RESEARCH DONE?

Some forms of scholarly or scientific research are accomplished in all colleges and universities. In the small liberal arts colleges it usually takes the form of pure research carried on as an adjunct of a professor's regular work. Traditionally such experimentation, investigation, or study is of secondary importance to the person's teaching responsibility.

In the large universities investigation usually takes the form of both pure and applied research. Heavy emphasis is placed on it, especially in the graduate and professional schools, in the natural and social sciences, and, because of the contracts available, through industry and the government.

Some research is carried on in the homes of the investigators;

other forms of inquiry are conducted in the offices, libraries, and laboratories of the institution; some types of research are handled off campus in the field and occasionally in the specialized libraries or particular laboratories of the organization contracting for the research.

HOW DOES RESEARCH VARY?

Although it is not immediately apparent, research differs markedly in different educational institutions. In the small, private liberal arts college, faculty members frequently undertake pure research on problems directly connected with their areas of specialization. Such projects usually have a close relationship to the academic activities in which the professor is involved. Occasionally such research is subsidized by the federal government, a philanthropic foundation, or a major corporation. However, in many cases the faculty member undertakes this research and study on his own time and at his own expense. Increasingly, talented undergraduates are asked to assist with the project, but generally the professor does his scientific experiments and scholarly study alone.

At the other end of the spectrum is the full professor at a prestigious Ivy League or state university. In these multiversities, productive research activity is accorded a very high priority by the institution, and consequently faculty members are much more concerned with their research than their teaching. Indeed, in some institutions, there are research professors who perform no teaching at all. However, most of the senior professors at the larger universities conduct considerable research and handle just one or two classes. Much of the research in the university is applied, as contrasted with the pure research of the small college faculty member. Although there is usually a connection between their extensive research and their limited teaching, sometimes there is not the remotest connection.

Of course the mission or type of institution will markedly affect the kind and extent of research carried on. In the public university—for example, the University of California at Berkeley—there will be an enormous amount of scientific and scholarly investigation underway in nearly every field and discipline. In an engineering school—for example, Massachusetts Institute of Technology—emphasis will be clearly placed on research in the scientific and technical areas. In a great private university—for example, the University of Chicago—research will be found in many areas, but especially in the social sciences and the humanities. In a college of education, quite naturally, there will be found many projects investigating areas of psychology and pedagogy; in a college of medicine, the research will be primarily on medical sciences and clinical practices; in a college of law, the research will be basically concerned with jurisprudence. And similar specialization occurs in all other professional schools in or out of the university.

ARE THERE RESEARCH-ORIENTED INSTITUTIONS?

Historians have proven conclusively that no college or university established prior to the twentieth century was chartered exclusively or even primarily for purposes of conducting research. However, during the past fifty years, and especially in the last twenty-five years, many of the great private institutions of higher learning and nearly all of the large state universities have become, at least in their graduate schools and professional colleges, what might be termed research-oriented institutions.

In studying this phenomenon we have not uncovered any comprehensive statistical reports indicating just how much money or

what percentage of professorial time goes into research as opposed to teaching. But it is obvious to even the most casual
observer that in distinguished institutions such as the University
of Illinois, Michigan State University, The Johns Hopkins University, Harvard University, and California Institute of Technology, an enormous amount of time and money is spent on
research.

There are, of course, several fine higher institutions around the
country that make no pretense of being true colleges or universities, even though they may carry on some limited teaching. Reference is made to such organizations as the Institute of Behavioral Sciences in California and the Institute for Advanced
Studies at Princeton. These are truly research-oriented institutions,
and any other programs they undertake are purely peripheral.

HOW IS RESEARCH FINANCED?

In the past, research—whether pure or applied—was financed
in many ways. That carried on in institutions of higher education
was supported by: (1) the individual researcher, (2) the institution, (3) a foundation, (4) the government, (5) a corporation,
(6) a wealthy individual, (7) a labor union or trade association,
or (8) a combination of some of these. However, since the late
1960's there has been an appreciable drying up of research funds
from these sources with a subsequent cutback of research activity
on many campuses.

In the small, private, liberal arts college, the faculty member
carries on his own research program without outside aid, but
often with the aid of a modest grant from the institution. The
current financial crisis in higher education has substantially limited the institutions' ability to provide this type of support for
faculty research. Philanthropic foundations, which have long

been a main source of support for university research projects, have been affected by changes in federal tax regulations governing foundations, and many are now actively supporting other causes and agencies in the society. Business and industrial organizations, which have been instrumental in providing for various forms of contract research for faculty members, are facing their own financial dilemma and are also cutting back on expenditures for research. State governments are looking very carefully at their financial support of higher education institutions as the voting public demands accountability from faculty, students, and administrators, in light of the campus unrest of recent years. And now the federal government, which had become the most generous dispenser of research funds for all colleges and universities, has changed the order of priority on the expenditure of its funds, resulting in the discontinuation of many established research programs and a definite decrease in the number of new projects being funded.

Although the immediate prospects for improvement in this picture are bleak, there is one positive outcome to this decrease in funds to support research activity. There are many professors with primary interests in research who, without funds to support their work, will have to justify their existence on the faculty by giving increased time and attention to their teaching responsibilities and their students. It is ironic indeed that the college professor's new interest in teaching, forced by the decrease in research funds, comes at a time when students and the public at large are demanding improvement in the teaching which takes place in our college and university classrooms. Thus we believe that the decade ahead will be a period in which the teaching and research function on the campus will be brought into a more favorable balance to the benefit of all of higher education.

HOW ARE RESEARCHERS TRAINED?

Persons engaged in scientific investigation and scholarly study —research *per se*—are trained in a variety of ways. Some have a natural inclination toward experimentation and the search for truth, and they start training themselves even as children. Others develop an interest in research techniques only after graduating from college, and they undertake their formal training later as graduate students. The majority of the research-oriented faculty members had a combination of early (informal) training and later (formal) training.

While research in different fields calls for different kinds of specific training, the basic undergirding for all scientific and scholarly investigation and exploration—whether in the library, the laboratory, or the field—is the development of the ability to think logically, objectively, and systematically about any problem. The scientific method and the scholarly approach to the solution of problems can be introduced at an early stage. Indeed, as one of the major aims of education, teaching students to think rationally is perhaps the first step in training them as researchers.

Although some of this early indoctrination toward research might come in high school, the real beginning should occur in undergraduate college, and the full measure of such training should be given in graduate or professional school. It is in these latter years that the student comes in contact with the senior professors engaged chiefly in research. Also it is in these advanced years of the master's and pre-doctoral activity that exposure to the techniques of scientific and scholarly research in classes and seminars, in the laboratories and libraries, occurs most frequently. Thus, while desirable ground work for a career in research might be laid in a liberal arts or general education curriculum, it probably will not achieve its zenith until the student enters a graduate or professional school at a university.

WHAT IS THE AMERICAN PH.D.?

The Doctorate of Philosophy is considered to be the highest academic degree that can be earned in this country. It is thought of as the passport for college teaching since its requirements generally include demonstrated mastery of a discipline, expertise in a segment of that discipline, a broad general background of education, and the ability to research and write constructively, if not creatively, on a particular project.

Unfortunately there are, as a rule, no requirements that a person taking a Ph.D. and planning a career in college teaching should have any exposure to the principles of pedagogy. Indeed, most of the emphasis in programs leading to the Ph.D. is on research, and herein lies one of the major weaknesses in the preparation of college teachers.

In response to the lack of emphasis on training for teaching in the traditional Ph.D. program, a number of new programs and approaches to preparing college professors have been suggested. One of the most noteworthy of these is the program leading to the Doctor of Arts degree. While stressing strong preparation in an academic discipline, this program also includes work preparing the candidate for teaching and changes the emphasis on the dissertation from straight research in the discipline to research related to teaching the discipline.[2]

A second area of emphasis in the Ph.D. program is on specialization. While the candidate is expected to be reasonably intelligent, and to have had a fairly broad liberal arts or general education, it is essential and imperative that he narrow down his interests to a specific discipline or even one facet of a discipline.

A third area of emphasis in the Ph.D. program is on vocationalism. In addition to the limiting of the scope of pre-doctoral studies, the candidates are forced to build their courses of study to aim at entry into and success in a particular vocation.

A fourth and final area of emphasis in the Ph.D. program is on professionalism. In addition to encouraging a narrow area of specialization and a particular vocational approach, the candidates are forced toward a mold of professionalism rather than encouraged to seek a full flowering of wisdom. This restraint, not generally found at the bachelor's or master's degree level, deserves careful scrutiny in the years ahead.

HOW IS RESEARCH INTEGRATED WITH TEACHING?

The majority of the thoughtful leaders in higher education—faculty, administrators, and trustees—agree that the first function of a college or university is the transmission of knowledge, commonly termed *teaching*. Many of these same leaders concur that the second function is the quest for knowledge, commonly termed *research*. Along with the transmission of information should go the stimulation of thinking; along with research should go its handmaiden, public service.

Some leaders see other functions for the university. Commager says, "Its functions are three-fold. First to transmit knowledge from one generation to the next. Second, to provide society with a body of trained professionals. Third, to expand the boundaries of knowledge through research and to discover new truths."[3]

Regardless of the secondary functions attributed to higher education, the two primary tasks of teaching and research prevail. And one of the most critical problems facing colleges and universities today and one which we referred to in the opening chapter is the determination of the proper relationship and the correct integration of teaching and research. And then, to make clear to the faculty, students, and other concerned parties exactly what this relationship will be.

We have made clear our feeling that the transmission of

knowledge—teaching—is the first and most important function of colleges and universities and is an activity in which faculty members must engage if they are to stay intellectually alive. One of the reasons why we and a host of other educators are inclined to this priority of values is simply that there is no better environment for teaching and learning than the well staffed, equipped, and administered college or university. Although these higher institutions also provide a desirable environment for research, there are other equally viable places for investigation, exploration, and experimentation.

Actually, the search for and the transmission of truth need not and should not be completely separated. The great teacher will not disdain scholarly study or scientific research even after he has achieved the pinnacle of success. By the same logic, the eminent research-oriented faculty member should want to pass along directly to the inquiring minds of students the fruits of his labor in laboratory or library. Discussing this relationship between research and teaching in the university, J. Douglas Brown, Provost and Dean of the Faculty, Emeritus, Princeton University, says, "Higher education in a university is a closely integrated continuum from which learning, teaching, and scholarship can be separated out as distinct elements only at the expense of the vitality of the total mission."[4]

WHAT ARE ITS PROBLEMS AND POTENTIALITIES?

The teaching function in many of the larger institutions has been so abused by the research-oriented professors that some drastic reforms are needed. For example, the most logical and direct method of integrating research and teaching is to agree that: (1) both are essential to the educational process, (2) both should be undertaken by educators at various times in their careers, and (3) each should have its proper recognition in terms of allocation of time, money, space, and staff. On point three, the policy of the institution should spell out quite clearly just what balance is expected for those professors handling teaching and research simultaneously. For example, if a distinguished teacher wishes only to teach, his wishes should be respected. Similarly, if an established scientist or scholar wishes only to conduct research, his wishes should be respected. In the latter instance, he should not be considered a member of the teaching faculty, he should not release his graduate assistants on unsuspecting students, and he should not be rewarded or promoted more generously than the great teacher.

The person desirous of and qualified for the optimum situation of combining research with teaching should be encouraged to conduct such research on his own time and be given the requisite means to accomplish this. Notice should be given that in a teaching institution, such as a college or university, teaching has priority over research, public service, consulting, or anything else.

No administrator denies the fact that brilliant advances brought about through research and reported in appropriate publications reflect credit on the sponsoring institution—and such credit is highly desirable. Nor would any educational executive discount the desirability of wealthy individuals, industrial corporations, philanthropic foundations, or government agencies becoming interested in his institution—such interest is highly desirable. But, most of the thoughtful administrators, plus a fair percentage of trustees and faculty members, have come to the realization that our colleges and universities are not doing an adequate teaching job in many areas due to the overemphasis on research. They see that students resent sloppy teaching, that parents wonder about questionable courses, and that donors object to the dilution of quality.

Properly integrated with teaching, research can make an enormous contribution to any higher institution. Not only does distinguished investigation reflect credit on the college or university, it also sharpens the educational offerings made to students, thus enhancing the entire curriculum.

DOCUMENTATION AND COMMENTARY

1. For a comprehensive treatment of the academician's rise to prominence resulting from the demand for his services as a researcher and the effect this has had on all of higher education, the reader is referred to Christopher Jencks and David Riesman, *The Academic Revolution*, Garden City, New York: Doubleday & Company, Inc., 1968.

2. For a more complete discussion of the Doctor of Arts degree the reader is referred to E. Alden Dunham, *Colleges of the Forgotten Americans*, New York: McGraw-Hill, Inc., 1969.

3. Henry Steele Commager, *The Saturday Review*, August 17, 1966, 13.

4. J. Douglas Brown, *The Liberal University: An Institutional Analysis*, New York: McGraw-Hill Book Co., 1969, 124.

3 SERVICE

There is a general agreement among the leaders in higher education that the universities have three major functions—teaching, research, and service to society. Although the smaller institutions emphasize teaching in greater proportion than research or external services, some of the latter are found operating in nearly every institution.

WHAT IS SERVICE?

Community, public, or external service in education refers to those programs and activities usually conducted off campus and indirectly connected to the institution's regular program of teaching and research. Some of these services are offered gratis or at cost to those benefiting from them. In this category of services are such diverse adjuncts to the university as medical and dental clinics, agricultural extension services, off-campus classes, and special cultural programs. Others include television and radio programs, repertory theatre, legal aid offices, tutorial services, and loan facilities in the institution's library.

Another type of service is faculty consulting, which is often arranged for and conducted by faculty members on their own time and for which there is a charge. During the past decade there has been a dramatic increase in this type of activity as agencies and other groups have realized that faculty members could help solve their problems. In this category are various forms of consultation to industry, government, and other organizations. In addition, many professors serve as lecturers, visiting consultants, and advisors to other colleges and universities and educational institutions.

In one sense, the athletic, social, and artistic programs sponsored by higher institutions, whether they require paid admissions or not, might be considered still another form of public services. Although private institutions are not subsidized with public funds for such services rendered, public institutions usually are so subsidized.

WHY IS SERVICE IMPORTANT?

Service is important for two over-riding reasons. First, the services related to higher education provide a testing ground for practical application of the lessons learned on a theoretical basis in the institution. Second, the services constitute a significant intellectual, spiritual, and recreational contribution from the university and help the institution meet its social commitment to society. For both reasons, universities have developed and expanded programs of services.

However, the guidelines for offering a service are that it should be related to the regular curriculum of the institution and be needed or desired by the community. When faculty propose offering specialized services to the public that have no relationship to the on-going program of the university, it is highly questionable that the institution should sponsor them. Such services, if needed, should be sponsored under other than institutional auspices.

Additionally, if the public does not need or desire certain university services, they should be phased out. No attempt should be made to foist off on the community educational or cultural programs merely to sustain and support particular programs or persons within the institution. Unfortunately, however, this advice often falls on deaf ears, as universities typically are not good at discontinuing once-useful programs which have lost their effectiveness and no longer serve a constructive purpose.

WHY ARE FACULTY MEMBERS INVOLVED?

Faculty members are involved in service because the implementation of such programs requires professional personnel. Generally these programs demand experts to operate them, and frequently they are directly related to the teaching and research that professors are doing. Thus, it is logical that faculty members, and occasionally administrators, are the primary staffers for service projects. Typical examples of such faculty involvement are professors of medicine participating in hospital and community clinics, professors of education serving as advisors to local school districts, and professors of economics and sociology serving as private consultants to industry and government. Recent developments include having faculty teams, composed of architects, urban affairs experts, and engineers, help cities with long-range planning, designing of structures for multi-purpose use, and developing complex transportation systems.

In addition to the use of faculty members and occasionally administrators, students are heavily involved in some services, especially those involving the local community. One illustration of such involvement is present in the essential nature of the medical and dental clinics. Were it not for these specific programs with clinical or public patients, it is doubtful that our medical and dental colleges could exist in their present form. Other community services students perform include operating day-care centers for children and working with the elderly and the poor through various social agencies.

WHERE DO SERVICES OCCUR AND HOW DO THEY VARY?

Community services generally occur in the large urban centers. An exception to this rule is found in the agricultural extension programs of the rural areas, and the recreational (athletic and aesthetic) programs offered by small colleges in small towns.

Clinical needs for medical colleges are such that the variety of illness and disease found in big cities is essential for their proper teaching and research functions. To some extent this same principle holds true for law schools in that visits to the various courts, participation in legal, political and corporate affairs, and voluntary services to legal aid offices require urban environs.

By the same token, field exercises, practical experience, and community services in such schools as forestry, marine biology, agriculture, mining, and veterinary medicine require quite different localities from the crowded cities because they deal with natural environments and animals in rural or wild settings. Thus, we find that there are sizable differences in the rural versus the urban community services.

Services offered by different types of higher institutions may also vary greatly. As mentioned earlier, the oldest and most familiar public services rendered by universities in the cities of this nation are probably the medical and dental clinics. It is hard to conjecture just how the indigent of the urban area or the budding young doctors could exist without the ever-present medical and dental clinics. In recent years, these services have been complemented by the efforts of professional schools, such as law, education, and social work, performing tasks in a variety of areas.

Also, as mentioned earlier, the most familiar public services rendered by the land-grant (tax-supported) colleges in the farming and ranching areas are probably the agricultural extension and county-agent programs. One of the reasons why our agricultural efforts have proven so successful is the close connection between the farmer and the state college or university. And now in highly populated areas where the growth of large suburbs is fast using up what rural areas and open space remain, these same services are being used to help property owners establish good lawns, to plant trees and shrubs, and to generally help maintain the quality of the land around them.

It is nearly axiomatic that all professional schools need the kind of practicum that public services programs offer. Colleges of journalism need proximity to the media for communication; colleges of education need local school systems for practice teaching; colleges of business need exposure to the market place for ideas and experience.

The newest and fastest growing addition to the higher education scene is the publicly supported community colleges, and many of them offer an unlimited number of services to the communities in which they are located. In fact, some are established with the philosophy that it is their role to perform any service the community requests, provided it is physically possible to do so.

WHAT ARE CONSULTATION SERVICES?

Most of the professional consultation rendered by faculty members is a kind of personal community service somewhat apart from the university. It is only natural that when executives in industry or government are faced with perplexing problems they should seek experts from institutions of higher learning. Thus they turn to faculty members who have established reputations in their respective fields. They employ these professors on a negotiated basis, usually part-time and quite apart from the college or university.

Consultation assignments in business and industry usually pay quite well; similar assignments with government or the foundations pay somewhat less well, but better than the college or university. In addition to the extra remuneration, which is always welcome, faculty members enjoy serving as consultants because such assignments provide a change of pace from campus and are professionally stimulating.

During the period following the successful launch of Sputnik, the professors in greatest demand as consultants to both the government and business were professors of science and engineering. A close second to them were the professors of business and economics. However, as national priorities changed, so did the demand for specialists. Now the greatest demand is for consultants who can work on the problems of the cities, including poverty and minority group concerns, who can solve ecological and environmental problems, and who are familiar with educational problems and deficiencies in our schools. Consequently, professors from fields such as urban studies, sociology, psychology, biology, and education are increasingly in demand as consultants.

HOW ARE THESE PROGRAMS
ADMINISTERED?

Service programs are administered in several ways. Those that are directly related to the university's educational program, such as medical and dental clinics, are managed by the college or professional school providing the service. Those that are related to the university's extra-curricular offerings, such as athletics and musical programs, are directed by executive officers employed by the university. Those that are supported by foundation or government grants may be supervised by a project director or department chairman. Those that are private in orientation usually are administered by the individual professor who is serving as consultant or chief investigator of the study.

As a general rule, major programs for the public both on and off campus, such as extension services or intercollegiate athletics, operate under the jurisdiction of faculty committees or advisory boards. These supervisory groups offer a link between the campus and the community, provide a policy source for the director, and offer guidelines for relating the public service program to the regular educational program of the institution.

HOW ARE THESE PROGRAMS FINANCED?

College and university service activities are usually financed by one or a combination of the following sources: (1) state or federal subsidy, (2) foundation subventions, (3) gate receipts and ticket sales, (4) contracts from industry, and (5) tuition and fees from student participants.

In the past, government sources have provided a major portion of support for services, especially those connected with agriculture and ecology. Foundations have also been generous in their grants to major universities for specific programs of services and for experimental projects. Athletic events and theatre programs have been usually covered, at least in part, by gate and box office receipts. Industry contributed to services through contracts and through ear-marked gifts. Tuition and fees from students and others participating in such activities as extension courses and medical clinics helped to defray a portion of the costs of such services.

However, rarely have these sources paid for the entire cost of the service received. The university usually had to absorb some of the cost, but did so willingly, recognizing this as one of its contributions to society. However, as colleges and universities are faced with increasing hard times financially, many are questioning their ability to maintain, much less expand, such services. And to add to the dilemma, government and foundations funds to support educational services are also decreasing as these agencies and organizations turn their attentions to other problems. In the future each university will be forced of necessity to examine carefully those service activities it supports, eliminating those not essential to the institution and not serving a distinct purpose in society, and permitting to continue only those which have a significant contribution to make and which the institution can financially support. This is not to suggest that the university should discontinue its service function and thus abdicate its responsibility to society; rather it suggests that those services performed must be closely related to what the university sees as its goal or mission and that it must be financially feasible to offer them.

4 ADVISEMENT

Section One in this book is entitled *Functions of the Faculty*. It is composed of five chapters dealing with the major responsibilities of faculty members. These five functions, arranged in a descending order of importance, are teaching, research, service, advisement, and committee assignments.

Advisement in relation to the other four faculty functions listed above is less formal. It is advice given the student by a faculty member usually on matters directly concerned with course work and academic programs. Not to be confused with advisement is guidance, the act or function of providing advice or counsel—usually by a student personnel specialist—to a student. Guidance is generally connected with the student's overall problems as they border on his educational program.

Closely connected to both advisement and guidance are the student affairs department, the student health service, the problems of transfers, the potentialities of tutoring, and the factor of impersonality or lack of identity.

WHO ADVISES?

College professors have since time immemorial given generously of themselves to guiding the intellectual and personal growth of their students. In the past, they did this informally as a regular part of their teaching assignment. However, as colleges grew in size and subsequently assumed more responsibility for their students' non-academic development, professors were unable to provide advice and counsel in all the areas in which students needed help. Thus, the first professional student personnel services were established to assist students with their non-academic problems. Special graduate-level programs to prepare student personnel administrators were started, stressing the development of skills in areas such as counseling, testing, and human relations. But even with these new services the faculty continued to provide the students' academic advisement, including help on matters relating to selection of courses, progress in individual classes, and the developing of career plans. One notes with interest that although student personnel workers, who provide guidance in the non-academic areas, receive special training for their work, those who perform the equally, if not more important, academic advisement receive none on how to perform their task. This is another area in which the present method of training college faculty members is not adequately preparing them for the jobs they must perform.

WHAT RESULTS ARE SOUGHT?

The aim, then, of both faculty and student personnel services guidance is to enable the recipient to adjust and succeed as a well-rounded student and person. Faculty advisors and guidance personnel should work together, helping each student maximize his potential ability and thus make college as profitable an experience for him as possible.

The long-range result sought is that of graduating the kind of person who, armed with a sound academic background and supported by broad social and cultural understandings, can take his place and succeed in the complex world of tomorrow.

HOW ARE PSYCHOLOGICAL RELATIONSHIPS HANDLED?

When large numbers of young people are living together away from home and under what might be assumed as some academic or intellectual pressures, it is obvious that their psychological relationships, with each other and with older people on campus, must be carefully considered. Consideration of these relationships is the province of such student personnel specialists as the dean of students or director of counseling.

Living away from home, especially for freshmen, can cause some psychological problems that are best solved with professional assistance. Somewhat the same is true with respect to problems arising from academic pressures. While the former should definitely be handled by full-time staff members on the student personnel services staff, the latter may be handled by regular faculty members assigned as academic counselors.

There are innumerable kinds of psychological relationships that occur on campus, and not all necessarily require referral to the dean or the professional guidance staff. In some instance a sympathetic and understanding faculty member can be of great comfort and assistance to a student with a problem. At the present time, however, the average faculty member is not equipped to handle serious psychological problems, and when they occur the student should be referred to highly qualified personnel in one of the professional service areas, such as the health service, the dean's office, or the counseling center.

WHAT IS ACADEMIC AND
CAREER COUNSELING?

Apart from the above-mentioned psychological problems, and far more frequently seen, are those problems related to either the immediate academic program or the longer-range career situation. The former occur to some degree with nearly every student at some time in college. These are to be expected, and provision must be made to solve them.

Academic counseling involves both the faculty and student personnel services. The first such counseling is that provided by the admissions officer when he recruits students by presenting to them and discussing with them the range of academic offerings of the institution. The next occurs at registration when faculty members advise on just what course patterns and curricular sequence should be followed. The third occasion for academic advisement appears when a problem arises within the term, and this is usually handled first on an informal basis by the instructor or professor involved—perhaps later by the dean's office. A fourth example of academic counseling is that taking place when the student begins to specialize, to seek a major, or to plan for upper division or graduate study, this being provided by senior faculty, departmental chairmen, or the dean's office.

The University of California, which was thought to have excellent admissions and advisory programs because of its high-powered and highly paid faculty, like many other multiversities, has taken another look at itself. Charles Muscatine, a professor of English at Berkeley and chairman of its Academic Senate's Select Committee on Education says, "As things now stand, our method of (academically) advising students—and it's pretty much the same method as used at most big schools—is weak." His committee in its 228-page report says, in recommendation 13: "The advising system in the college of letters and science should be made largely voluntary through the adoption of such improvements as mechanizing the record keeping, reforming the orientation procedure, simplifying the rules and liberalizing their applications, providing ample printed materials, appointing specialists, promoting combinations of advising and teaching, and encouraging participation of student advisors."[1] Unfortunately, the University of California's experiences with advisement are not unlike those at far too many other colleges and universities today.

Career counseling is usually linked closely with upper-division academic counseling. It consists of planning the student's academic program in line with long-range professional or occupational goals. Faculty advisors, counseling specialists, and occasionally placement offices all share responsibility for career counseling, but the greatest impact may come from the faculty member. Support for this position is given by Feldman and Newcomb in their investigation of the impact of college on students. They reported, "Evidence is accumulating that faculty are particularly important in influencing occupation decisions and educational aspirations. In over a dozen studies in which students were asked to name the important sources of influence on their vocational planning and decisions, faculty along with parents ranked as extremely important. In fact, with only two or three exceptions, students perceived faculty to be either as influential as their parents or more so."[2]

WHO SUPERVISES INDIVIDUAL STUDY ACTIVITIES?

Closely connected with academic counseling and faculty advisement are efforts designed to assist students encountering problems in mastering their course work. These efforts frequently take the form of tutoring or special study. Such academic activities are usually conducted by faculty members, but sometimes upper division or graduate students also serve as tutors. Occasionally the guidance office will coordinate such efforts. Frequently this kind of extra educational effort is arranged by the student privately and quite apart from the regular program of the institution.

Another approach to learning which involves individual advising is independent study. As most commonly used, a student selects a project or topic not covered by regular courses and studies independently in this area under the direction of a professor. Independent study provides students the opportunity to be involved in planning their own education by selecting topics which interest them. Students also are able to pursue work at their own rate of learning speed.

Many college calendars are being revised to provide a special time for independent study because of the apparent advantages it has for some students over the traditional approach to course work and because of its popularity with students. Although it is still early to determine the value of such programs, especially when they involve large numbers of students, there are indications suggesting that one area of weakness in independent study is that faculty members do not know how, and in many instances do not care to take the time, to supervise their students. So what happens when a student enrolls in independent study is that he gets a vacation from formal class work, often conveniently arranged to take place off campus, and the faculty member gets more time for his research and writing.

WHAT IS THE TRANSFER PROBLEM?

Although it is not a major consideration to all faculty members, the problem of student transfers or articulation deserves consideration herein. The number of students changing from one institution of higher education to another continues to increase.

This trend will continue as the number of two-year colleges grows and as new upper-division colleges (junior and senior year only) are established to accommodate their graduates.

Our American system of higher education encourages students to change institutions more readily than in other countries. One reason for this is that they can make such changes frequently without penalty. Since most of our colleges and universities are regionally accredited, academic credits earned at one are accepted by others.

A problem arises in this matter of transfer when a student makes a change in mid-term. The educational and social adjustments of changing from one institution to another during the academic year can be difficult. Faculty members and student counselors must exhibit understanding and patience in smoothing out the transition.

Another problem especially acute for students of the two-year junior or community colleges is that of transferring to a senior or four-year institution. The enormous growth of junior colleges, from 277 with an enrollment of 55,000 in 1930 to 524 with 500,000 in 1960 to 1,091 with 2,500,000 in 1970, has generated a serious problem of volume which many senior colleges and universities are unable or unwilling to accept.

Extended and continuing articulation between junior and senior institutions has done much to solve these problems in many states. Further improvement will depend in large measure upon both junior and senior faculties exercising reasonable flexibility in terms of designing curricular models that will encourage and enable appropriate transfers within the academic superstructure.

HOW ARE SOCIOLOGICAL
RELATIONSHIPS HANDLED?

As in the case of psychological problems of students, those

arising on the social side can be serious and deserving of careful treatment by professionally trained personnel. Faculty members can provide a certain amount of help with some of these problems, but others will require deeper understanding and more time than faculty members have at their disposal. Thus, most colleges and universities have on the student personnel staff specially trained individuals to provide remedial measures as needed.

A considerable amount of helpful guidance is provided by the young faculty members and graduate students who serve as counselors in the dormitories. These people are immediately available, and can sometimes be more effective than professional counselors, since they are closer to the student's age (chronologically) and to the student's residence (proximity).

WHAT IS THE STUDENT AFFAIRS DEPARTMENT?

Faculty members usually are encouraged to participate in some, but not all, of the extra-curricular activities of the student body. They participate generally as spectators at athletic, social, or cultural events. However, in the smaller colleges they are sometimes called upon to supplement the work of the specialists in the student affairs department.

As such, they may be asked to provide help with extra-curricular counseling of various kinds. Most prominent among these assignments are those of advising student clubs, government, and recreational activities. In days past, faculty members were used as coaches for athletic teams, but now such positions are filled by professional athletic coaches and physical education experts.

The student affairs department is the administrative division charged with the responsibility of advising and assisting the students with activities other than academic activities. As Charles Bursch has said, variety of structure is a characteristic of this staff division, but all identifiable services can be grouped under: "student welfare services, student activities services, and student control services."[3]

Generally the person in charge is called the *dean of students* or *director of student affairs*. Student welfare services involve such psychological programs as testing and counseling, scholarships and financial aid, and part- and full-time placement. Student activities services involve extra-curricular and co-curricular activities such as student government, and social, recreational, cultural, and athletic programs. Student control services involve such custodial functions as housing, feeding, and campus discipline.

WHAT IS THE ROLE OF THE STUDENT HEALTH SERVICE?

As mentioned above, historically administrators and faculty members handled not only the curricular programs on campus, but the extra-curricular as well. Depending upon one's definition of student health services, the function of keeping the students healthy might be considered extra-curricular. In any case, regular faculty members no longer find themselves serving in this area except under emergency conditions. Most institutions now have a medical doctor as director of the student health services. In addition, there is usually one or more round-the-clock nurses serving in the college infirmary. Some universities have large staffs, frequently including specialists, such as psychiatrists, on call.

Among the problems with which the student health service must advise and assist are academic overwork and fatigue, drug use and abuse, pre-marital sex and birth control, and lack of aims and goals, often associated with a student's search for individual identity. Faculty members may recognize these and other problems through such symptoms as a sudden drop in grades, excessive absences, withdrawal tendencies, and poor general health. When this occurs, every effort should be made to have the student see competent medical authorities in the health services.

ARE THERE PROBLEMS OF IMPERSONALITY?

Faculty members are justifiably critical of the bureaucracy of the multiversity. Not only are the students seemingly reduced to IBM cards, but even full professors are submerged by the sheer weight of numbers. Student personnel administrators in particular regret that as institutions expand in size and complexity the people within them fail to stand out as individuals endowed with identifiable personalities.

But when this occurs, the teaching faculty have a special responsibility to humanize their relationships with students to the fullest extent possible. In addition, the faculty member is presented with an opportunity to influence the young people that he counsels along other than purely academic lines. While he is not expected to radically change the character of a student, he is expected to provide, by discussion if not by example, some guidelines of value.

While there is much to be said for the use of an iconoclastic approach to certain scholarly pursuits, the opposite approach might prove most helpful in terms of helping students solve social and personality problems. Even the most brilliant intellectual or the most suave sophisticate at age twenty can profit from the kind of reasoned logic or warm common sense that should be given by faculty members when needed by students.

It is recognized that not every instructor or professor can successfully play the role of old Mr. Chips, but none should be given faculty status as a teacher if he is unable or unwilling to communicate, to relate, to counsel his students at least informally and unofficially. And to help insure that those who teach in college have the capacity to relate to students in this manner, the Ph.D. programs, which most complete in preparation for teaching, should give some attention to developing an understanding of human relations and should provide the prospective faculty member with the opportunity to gain experience in advising.

DOCUMENTATION AND COMMENTARY

1. Charles Muscatine in *College Management*, May, 1967.

2. Kenneth A. Feldman and Theodore M. Newcomb, *The Impact of College on Students*, Vol. 1, San Francisco: Jossey-Bass, Inc., 1969, 252-253.

3. Charles W. Bursch in Gerald P. Burns, ed., *Administrators in Higher Education*, New York: Harper and Row, Publishers, 1962, 142.

5 COMMITTEE ASSIGNMENTS

Committee assignments can be classified along with death and taxes as being inevitable concomitants of a professor's life. They are boring, time-consuming, and important, and professors complain about them continuously, protesting that they are the chief obstacles that keep them from getting at their really important work. And yet if a considerate administration proposes to remove certain problems of institutional life from committee consideration, the professors immediately and loudly object.

WHAT IS PROFESSIONAL PARTICIPATION?

There are two alternatives: a heavy committee load which consumes much faculty time, but which gives the faculty appropriate professional participation in the running of the institution; and a light committee load which permits faculty members to concentrate on their own professional and teaching duties, but which gives them very little to say about institutional matters. The former, in our opinion, is to be preferred even though it is a more costly process in both time and money. It makes the faculty a part of the college's management, which in turn leads to a more smoothly run institution based on faculty knowledge that it is playing a part in charting the course of the overall enterprise.

The selection of this alternative, however, is valid only if the faculty is operating at a genuine professional level. If it is engaging in faculty politics and using the committee system to promote political rather than professional ends, obviously a different decision must be made by the administration.

There are several kinds of faculty committees, and they can be classified by structure and function. Structurally, there are three general types. First, those which are appointed by the administration; second, those which are elected by the faculty; and third, those which are mixed in composition, containing both faculty-elected members and administrative appointees.

The structure is often adapted to the kind of job the committee is doing. For an administration-centered project, such as the development of a special program to meet current needs of regional industry, an administration-appointed committee might be the best. For a problem involving professional ethics or the judgment of a faculty member by his peers, clearly an elective approach is to be preferred. For advice and counsel in the appointment of major administrative officers, a mixed committee involving the perspectives of both specialists and generalists might serve most effectively.

WHAT ARE THE FUNCTIONS
OF COMMITTEES?

Committees must also be classified according to function. Most faculties have a curriculum committee of one sort or another, a committee dealing with faculty and staff affairs and benefits, and a committee dealing with professional ethics. More recently, particularly in the larger public systems and institutions of higher education, faculties have taken an increasing interest in the budget and often have a special committee for the purpose of keeping watch over administration policies in this regard. In some cases, and particularly in California where the faculty is very close to politics, a legislative committee is also part of the organizational scheme.

The emphasis on student relationships has only recently been recognized by faculty committees. One outgrowth of the recent student activism on campus has been a rising student demand to be included in policy-making at an institutional level. In response, the majority of colleges and universities today have established more faculty committees devoted to student affairs and have arranged for student representation on committees traditionally reserved for faculty.

The faculties' function in curriculum and program deserves special mention. Elsewhere in this volume there is a discussion of the competition between faculty and administration in the designing of curriculum and program. Suffice it to say here, however, that the faculty plays a most important role in this area, and this should be continued.

ARE THERE COMMITTEE LIMITATIONS?

There are certain limitations, however, within which the faculty must operate even in this area of its primary concern. One is the trustees' delimitation of the mission of the institution. No faculty committee or senate should have the right to propose programs which change the course of the institution away from the mission as set forth by the responsible trustees. A second frame of reference is fiscal reality. The faculty should take into account the number of dollars available when determining how simple or how complex a program should be. A third compelling factor is the necessity to place the interests of the institution above the interests of the individual. Far too many faculties plot programs and departmental schedules which allow every individual to ride his professional hobby horse. Sometimes in a large institution this turns out to be possible more often than not, but it leads to undue and unfortunate course proliferation which has deleterious effects on the budget and on the entire teaching program.

If a faculty operates within these guidelines and thoroughly accepts them, there is no reason why the making of curriculum cannot be finally delegated to it. Far too often, however, the concept of delegation implies to many faculty members the overriding of trustee decisions and an unreal approach to fiscal problems.

Part of the control of program which is customarily delegated to the faculty is the structuring of requirements for degrees. There is, after all, no better judge of the appropriate meaning of the degree, whether at the associate's, bachelor's, master's, or doctoral level than the faculty members who have created and organized the program leading to it. Here again certain doctrines of reasonableness must prevail. A musician, for instance, who wants a 124-unit bachelor's program to consist of 90 units in his department, obviously is not operating with the best interest of the institution or the student at heart. The counsels of the specialist must always be merged with the counsels of the generalist, the administrator, and the final policymaker—the trustee. However, faculty members should have much to say about the creation of degree requirements. So also should they have final word in determining who should and who should not receive the degrees whose programs they have structured. The vote of the faculty on candidates for degrees may seem to be an annual ritual with little meaning. Actually, however, it should have the most profound significance and should be taken quite seriously by both faculty and administration.

WHAT ABOUT STUDENT PARTICIPATION?

As mentioned earlier in this chapter, one outgrowth—and we believe a positive one—of the recent period of student unrest has been the students' desire to have more say about their own education through participation in institutional decision making. One way this is accomplished is through committee membership.

There are a number of substantive and controversial issues involved when considering student membership on committees charged with the responsibility of managing a college and its programs. One question is whether students can be held responsible for their decisions to a degree commensurate with the authority committee membership gives. Other questions are whether students have the expertise and maturity of judgment to perform adequately in this role, whether such a transient group should make decisions and establish policy which may affect the next generation of students more than themselves, and whether students have the time and sustained interest to become involved in the inner workings of college management.

These arguments not withstanding, students are increasingly being invited to join committees, and perhaps what is more important is that they are being heard. Some of the positions students now hold include memberships on boards of trustees, university-wide senates, school and department committees for establishing requirements and courses, search committees seeking both new administrators and faculty members, and committees for evaluating the performance of these administrators and faculty members after their selection.

Like many other changes which have recently taken place in higher education, it is too early to tell what the overall effect of student committee membership will be. However, it is clear that in those areas of greatest personal concern to students, such as establishing social and living regulations and dealing with discipline, they have a very valuable contribution to make. However, on matters dealing with promotion and tenure considerations, student contributions should generally not exceed making recommendations on what they perceive a faculty member's effectiveness to be.

Although there are no fixed rules which can adequately determine the nature and extent of student committee membership appropriate for every college, administrators and faculty alike should recognize that students do have a contribution to make. And, when committee membership is planned so it is part of the total learning experience, student involvement in decision making can be both a satisfying and profitable experience for both college and student.

HOW DO ADVISORY COMMITTEES OPERATE?

Returning to our classification of committees, there are two roles which committees can play on a faculty—one is advisory and the other is that of a committee with delegated power or authority. Currently there is a strong urge on the part of many faculty members to change their advisory role on committees into one possessing fully delegated authority. This carries with it a good many problems. We discuss this matter later from another perspective, but here let us say that there are certain roles which a faculty can play effectively, having to do with curriculum and personnel, in which the delegation of authority is quite possible and appropriate.

However, whether or not such authority should be delegated depends on certain factors which must be carefully evaluated by both the faculty and the administration. Chief among these factors is the professional competence of the faculty. A faculty which consists largely of young people fresh from graduate school, unmellowed by experience and lacking the perspective which long years of teaching provide, is not a faculty which can utilize delegated authority to the best effect.

Also the goals of those who demand faculty authority through delegation deserve thorough examination. If the goals are professional in nature—which means that they fit within the frames of reference set by the governing board, the legally established mission of the institution, and realism in terms of the fiscal assets and potential of the college or university—then delegated authority becomes genuinely possible.

HOW ARE POTENTIALITIES OF COMMITTEES DETERMINED?

The effectiveness of committees and what can be done to make them more efficient is a subject in and of itself. Everyone has heard the hoary jokes—a camel is an animal so awkward and ungainly he must have been created by a committee; or, another, a committee is a group of the unqualified appointed by the uninterested to do the unimportant. If faculty committees are properly formed, skillfully led, and effectively utilized, they can make significant contributions to their institutions. If an administration provides the inspiration and encouragement needed, they can achieve these results much more rapidly and helpfully than otherwise.

A basic principle is that if a committee is to produce optimum results, it should be kept as small as possible. A large committee might be effective in producing a study, the various complex parts of which are allocated to certain members of the committee. But if the job requires action, such as a resolution to be presented within the foreseeable future, then the smaller the committee the better.

A second requirement for a committee operation is staff help. This may be as simple as allocating a part-time typist to turn out the committee's reports so this will not be a responsibility of the professional members, or it may require arrangements for use of a computer or a small research staff. In any case, the fundamental principle here is that professors should profess and not have to do clerical work, and this especially applies to committee assignments.

A third requisite for making a committee effective is to give the members of the committee the conviction that what they are doing is important. If they are certain that their recommendations will be seriously considered, even if not wholly accepted, and will contribute to the solution of the problem under advisement, then the morale and approach of the committee will be sound. Committees should not be given irrelevant and insignificant assignments just to keep the membership busy; everyone's time in a good college or university is so valuable that this type of administrative device should be abandoned.

HOW IS COMMITTEE ORGANIZATION AND OPERATION ARRANGED?

In some large institutions there are developing what might be called "career committeemen" on the faculties. These individuals are seldom outstanding teachers or researchers. They seem to gain their occupational satisfactions from academic politics, rather than from either their classroom or their professional disciplines. In fact, the creation of a group of academic politicians is very easy in a large institution, although only a relatively small number of individuals are willing to assume this type of responsibility on a continuing basis. Most professors would much rather conduct research, teach classes, and stay away from academic committees. But, there are always a few who enjoy such activities and who participate regularly to the extent they are regularly called on by their colleagues for such assignments.

These career committeemen sometimes hurt, rather than help, the less articulate faculty members they are allegedly representing. If the concept of faculty participation in academic policy making and professorial guidance is to remain valid, it should be total faculty participation through broad representation, not partisan participation engineered by a small group of faculty politicians. The latter frequently slight their teaching responsibilities and become, in effect, pseudo-administrators with a self-seeking point of view. Certain devices exist which can prevent such a development or at least keep it from getting out of hand. One of these is to limit the terms of faculty members on academic senates or committees; another is to permit a faculty member to have only one committee assignment per year; another is to prevent repetition of membership by the same individual on certain committees.

One additional means of improving the quality of faculty participation on committees is for faculty in training to observe and participate in committee work as part of their preparation for a college position. The careful reader has already observed that a consistent and underlying theme of this book is the need for change in the traditional approach to preparing college teachers (i.e., the research oriented Ph.D. degree program). To this end it is suggested that an internship in college teaching would be a welcome addition to the training program for prospective professors. Ideally, such an internship would not be concerned only with classroom teaching, but rather would give an exposure to all the things a college professor does—including committee work.

A second characteristic of faculty committees—almost universal in its application—is their tendency to concentrate on procedures rather than on substance. For some reason, the faculty mind, when it becomes involved in its own politics, is totally bemused by the necessity for care and caution in approaching the group solution of its problems. As a result, it is very easy for an excellent committee system to bog down under the weight of its own operational minutiae. It is essential for certain individuals—preferably other faculty members, but if these are not available, then administrators—to keep reminding the faculty constantly that it must stick to the point and deal with the substantive concerns before it. Otherwise months and even years can be wasted in procedural and parliamentary wheel-spinning.

Faculty committees are an integral and vital part of the academic scene. They can be and should be important and useful devices to bring about solutions to academic problems. Despite the many hurdles which must be surmounted if they are to achieve effective operation, they are worth the time and effort necessary because of their potentialities for providing positive and helpful influence in academic government. The growth and development of American higher education is dependent upon such professional influence, and it is best exerted through faculty committees.

SECTION TWO

Building the Faculty

INTRODUCTION TO SECTION TWO

Just as Section One of this book dealt with the five primary functions of the faculty, this section deals with the five major activities undertaken by institutions in building the faculty. While there may be more than these five considerations involved in the process of deciding upon, obtaining, and orienting a new faculty, these are certainly the most important.

The verb building *is deliberately used to introduce these efforts because it describes most accurately what transpires in this essential aspect of higher education. Moving from one step to another, we start with the premise that we cannot have a faculty until we know what kind and what numbers of people we want. Thus, the first consideration is philosophical—what sort of institution is desired and what curriculum concepts will make it that way.*

Having determined the purpose of the college and outlined the interacting disciplines that will serve that purpose, we are ready to determine what courses or subjects should be offered within the curriculum. Hand in hand with course determination goes the decision on what pedagogical methods will be employed to present this subject matter.

The third step is that of exploring what channels, agencies, and opportunities exist for selecting and evaluating the kinds of teachers needed. The selection procedure, initially and throughout the life of the college, is vitally important to the obtaining and retaining of the right type, size, and caliber of faculty.

Recruitment procedures follow closely upon the heels of selec-

tion procedures. The latter are the philosophical and theoretical beginnings to employment, and the former are the practical and mechanical procedures to such employment.

The final consideration in this section is that covered in Chapter 10, "Orientation Procedures." In that chapter are described some of the latest and most effective ways and means of educating, training, or counseling the faculty to achieve each person's fullest potential and to attain the aim, goals, and objectives of the institution.

6 CURRICULUM CONCEPTS

Before an institution can proceed to select, recruit, and orient a faculty, it must make some judgments about what kind of institution it wants to be. These judgments will deal with philosophical considerations regarding the curriculum of the college or university. They will be followed by practical considerations bearing upon the disciplines or courses that will comprise the curriculum and the who, what, where, and when of faculty participation. Professor Drucker, in discussing reasons for an orderly curriculum, notes that, "No discipline can lengthen a man's arm. But it can lengthen his reach by hoisting him on the shoulders of his predecessors. Knowledge organized in a discipline does a good deal for the merely competent; it endows him with some effectiveness. It does infinitely more for the truly able; it endows him with excellence."[1]

WHAT IS THE CURRICULUM?

The curriculum is sometimes thought of as everything that impinges upon a student in an academic setting. A more narrow definition, and one that receives greater usage, is that of the curriculum's being the academic program of the institution. A third meaning for the term is that a curriculum is a group of scholarly disciplines composed of courses in related subject-matter fields.

Regardless of the definition used, the curriculum or curriculums of a college or university comprise the program of studies that is offered. In the small, liberal arts college the curriculum is usually composed of courses in the humanities (such as English, languages, classics, and art), in the physical sciences (such as mathematics, physics, chemistry, and biology), and in the social sciences (such as history, sociology, anthropology, psychology, and philosophy).

There is no hard and fast rule as to precisely what disciplines or subjects must fall within the usual three academic divisions of the typical undergraduate college. Indeed, there is considerable difference of opinion among leading educators as to whether the curriculum should emphasize general or liberal education.

In the technical, professional, or specialized institutions, such as schools of engineering, law, or medicine, the curriculum is narrowed to those subjects most germane to producing a graduate highly proficient in a particular discipline. Generally these curriculums are on the graduate level and taken up only after completion of four years in a general or liberal, broad curriculum, undergraduate college.

In the large university there are many colleges, and as a rule, each has its own curriculum. Frequently there are a small number of undergraduate schools, such as the liberal arts and science college, the school of general studies, and the extension division. In addition, and building upon these divisions with a broad, general, or classical curriculum, is the upper division composed of several graduate and professional divisions, such as the graduate school of arts and sciences, college of education, and the school of business.

WHAT IS ITS HISTORY?

The curriculum or academic program in higher education began informally with Socrates, his predecessors, and followers, strolling about the Groves of Academe, or seated together in a temple, with a small number of students, asking and answering questions from a broad spectrum of fields. The Academy of Plato and the Lyceum of Aristotle may have formalized the courses of study to some extent, but historians agree that the curriculum, as a series of formal and related subjects for discourse and study, did not appear until the early universities were formed.

The medieval universities began the organization of learning with the use of the printing press and the identification of the curriculum. The latter was divided into two parts. The *trivium* (composed of grammar, logic, and rhetoric) and the *quadrivium* (composed of arithmetic, music, geometry, and astronomy). The early universities of the Western World, such as Bologna, Padua, Salerno, Paris, Oxford, and Cambridge, expanded on these subjects, especially with the introduction of languages.

Most institutions of higher education in both Europe and America maintained a fixed or classical curriculum until the latter half of the nineteenth century. Although European universities still follow much the same rigid pattern, Harvard initiated, and other American institutions quickly adopted, what has come to be known as the elective system of general education. As documented earlier, this went hand-in-hand with the rise of the natural sciences and the emergence of departmentalism; it contributed to the now burgeoning problem of course proliferation and narrow specialization.

The system of education which dominates today's universities, while far less narrow than a century ago, is still largely irrelevant to the interest and needs of many undergraduates. Indeed, the irrelevance of both the curriculum and courses, as well as the previously mentioned poor quality of much teaching, is a topic which students and others are calling to the attention of administrators. Fortunately, most universities are taking seriously these expressions of student concern, and reforms are taking place. Today in many institutions program requirements are being reviewed, new courses (including some proposed by students) are being developed, and new approaches to courses, such as minicourses, are being suggested. Although there is understandably some resistance to these changes, especially in the more conservative institutions and on the part of some faculty members, those favoring a liberalizing of the curriculum believe progress is being made and are optimistic regarding continued improvement in the future.

WHO DETERMINES THE CURRICULUM?

The determination of the curriculum is a responsibility of the faculty. The instructors and professors are the persons intimately related to the course work by virtue of teaching the classes and directing the seminars. They are also closer to the expressed needs of the students for various modifications of the disciplines. And, finally, the faculty is professionally geared to handling the total educational program of the institution, and the curriculum is the core of that program.

However, as Beardsley Ruml and many other leaders in the field have observed, the faculty is not the only group with a genuine interest in curricular affairs. The *students,* as the learners exposed to class, laboratory, and library assignments, are important partners in all the processes pertaining to the curriculum.

The *administration,* as the arrangers of the college calendar, the academic facilities, and the overall educational program, has a supervisory relationship. The *trustees,* as the governing body of the institution, while not intimately connected with the course content of laboratory experiments, have the final policy jurisdiction over all activities of the institution.

Thus, while we feel that the faculty should have primacy in curricular matters, it should by no means be exclusive. When other responsible voices are heard along with the faculty, in determining the courses that shall be taught, the final product is well balanced and even the faculty is better served than if it alone made all the decisions in this sensitive area.

WHAT ARE THE BASIC CONCEPTS OF CURRICULUM?

There are several fundamental principles involved in the curriculum. As generally defined, it refers to the total academic program of a college or university. As specifically defined, it refers to the particular subjects or disciplines, classes or courses, and educational emphasis of the institution.

One of the main considerations of the curriculum is to offer the students that academic feast that the institution purports to present. It is at this point that the governing board has a major responsibility. Not only must the board provide resources for the physical implementation of the curriculum (plant, faculty, administration, and students), but it has a legal responsibility to provide the kind of educational program for which the institution was chartered.

A second important concept is that the curriculum should emphasize quality rather than quantity. In other words, it is better to have one hundred good courses than two hundred poor ones.

There is sometimes a tendency on the part of faculties, and especially strong departments, to insist on offering specialized courses that are of interest to the teacher, but not essential to the overall curriculum of the school. This proliferation of courses is not only unproductive educationally, but financially very expensive as well. Many universities can trace part of the current financial dilemma they now face to the unwise planning of course offerings. Thus, the academic administrators (department chairmen, deans, and even presidents) must provide patient and restrained, but firm and flexible leadership in balancing need with desire.

A third basic consideration is that the faculty should provide major leadership and the administration should provide a light touch in determining not only the content of the curriculum but the decision on who shall present the courses. This aspect of curricular affairs impinges on both the faculty's right to determination of subject matter and the administration's right to determination of personnel. Therefore, the wise faculty members and the skilled administrators recognize the need of sharing ideas and decisions in this gray area, as well as the desirability of including student recommendations in their deliberations.

A final precept is that the curriculum, as the basic activity of any educational institution, takes precedence over all other programs on campus. While few experienced educators would dispute the value of co-curricular activities, such as artists in residence, or extra-curricular activities, such as student government, nearly all concur that the academic program must come first in any consideration affecting the institution.

There are times in the history of every institution when the favorite pastime becomes the revision of the curriculum. The improvement of the curriculum should be a constant concern of faculty members. If it is, then the faculty, individually and collectively, are strategically positioned to refute unfounded charges from any source that the curriculum is moribund, too liberal, too conservative, or irrelevant. When legitimate changes are needed and desired, they should be brought about jointly by the faculty and administration, in consultation with students, with the trustees being advised of the changes and the reasons for them. The scissors-and-paste method of revising the curriculum is still in vogue at a few of the smaller institutions, but most institutions now approach this important task by employing modern group procedures that place emphasis on legitimate needs of the students.[2]

WHO TEACHES THE CURRICULUM?

The curriculum is taught by the faculty. *Faculty* is a generic term referring to teachers, although in some large state and urban universities it includes persons with faculty rank who are not teachers. Reference is made to distinguished scientists employed solely to conduct research, or artists in residence who merely create, or experts in agronomy who consult off campus.

The teaching faculty in a small college is usually employed on a full-time basis and devotes the bulk of its time to teaching regular classes. The teaching faculty in a large university is usually composed of both part-time and full-time teachers. Arguments can be presented in favor of, and opposed to, the employment of other than regular or full-time teachers.

The classic stance of the proponents for full-timers only is that they develop undivided loyalty and dedication to their institution, its curriculum, and its students. The case against the employment of full-timers is both educational and economical. Educationally there is some advantage—especially in the professional schools, such as medicine and law—in bringing in different (part-time) practitioners who are actually doing what they are teaching. Economically there is some advantage in using part-timers because they are frequently leaders in their field whose salaries could not be matched by the university.

Another view of the teaching faculty is the usual division by rank within a college or university. Traditionally there has been and still are four ranks—instructor, assistant professor, associate professor, and full professor. Some institutions vary the lower ranks by including tutors and/or lecturers. And some institutions, particularly the large affluent universities, vary the upper ranks by including distinguished professors and/or professorships named for a chair donated by a wealthy person.

Occasionally teaching is carried on by other than regular faculty members. In recent years there has been considerable criticism of some of the larger institutions that assign teaching assistants and graduate assistants to this task. This frequently happens when a distinguished professor is too tied up in his research, writing, or consulting to meet his classes regularly. Some of these pinch-hitters turn out to be more proficient teachers than their senior colleagues, but usually the students are once again the victims of the system.

Since most academic administrators—deans and presidents—have served some time as faculty members, it is logical that some of them may wish to continue with a reduced teaching load. And, frequently they are excellent teachers. However, the problem they face is the pressure of time and travel that occasionally takes them from their scheduled classes.

One of the most effective groups of sometime college teachers is the visiting resource people invited sporadically as special lecturers. These are frequently leaders in the community who have distinguished themselves in some field of interest to the class, and they usually provide an interesting and exciting period within certain courses. Unfortunately the use of such visitors is often limited to the urban institutions because of proximity to such specialists. However, the rural institutions attempt to counter this by inviting outstanding practitioners in the arts, sciences, and other fields for both curricular and co-curricular special events and all-college convocations.

HOW IS THE CURRICULUM ADMINISTERED?

The academic program of the institution is usually organized into individual units such as colleges, divisions, and departments. Occasionally, a university will have "faculties of" rather than "colleges of," and frequently a college will have either divisions or departments.

As the chief executive officer of the institution, the president or chancellor is the academic leader of the entire enterprise. In a large university, he is somewhat removed from the curriculum and leaves its administration to a provost or academic vice president, plus the several college deans. In a small college, the president is usually involved in the academic administration, although the dean is the key figure.

The details of curriculum management, supervision, and co-ordination are generally left to the department chairmen or division heads. The intricacies of curriculum policy formulation, below the level of the president and board, are the responsibility of the faculty and usually are handled by the faculty senate, the academic council, the educational affairs committee, or a similar body.

Since teachers and scholars value highly their professional status and are sensitive about administrative interference, able educational executives, whether presidents, deans, or department heads, use a light touch in providing leadership in this realm. However, these executives or administrators have an important responsibility actively to advise, assist, and even supervise the instructors and professors engaged in operating the curriculum.

HOW IS THE CURRICULUM ORGANIZED?

The educational program of the institution is usually organized so that related subject matter or scholarly disciplines are in the same college, division, or department. One of the serious charges made and frequently substantiated against colleges and universities is that no logical order is visible in the organization and structuring of the curriculum. The critics claim that the academic programming is left entirely to the whim of the faculty and that pressures emerge that cause unnecessary proliferation of the curriculum.

Students of academic affairs and other curriculum experts hold that stronger leadership is long over-due on the part of deans and department chairmen. It is claimed that if such leadership were available more interdisciplinary courses would result, fairer teaching loads would occur, fewer fragmented subjects would be offered, and thus higher faculty salaries could be paid. Fortunately, and in part due to the current financial crisis in higher education, some improvements are being made in these areas.

Although there has been much justifiable criticism of the Parsons College philosophy, some salutary steps have been pioneered at that benighted institution. Millard Roberts, the controversial former president, lowered admission standards, reduced the course offerings, provided extensive tutoring, raised the tuition, and enormously increased professional salaries ($40,000 top). It is obvious to every educator that schools and colleges cannot be operated strictly along the lines of a business or industry. However, it is possible to operate with academic efficiency if the economics of careful curricular management are used.

WHAT EXTERNAL AGENCIES INFLUENCE
THE CURRICULUM?

There are many off-campus groups that exert varying influences on the academic programs of our higher institutions. Some of these pressures are constructive and some are destructive.

The alumni, as might be expected, are a vocal and frequently effective group influencing the curriculum. There are many reasons for bringing pressure to bear and many ways in which they do it.

The old grads are usually in favor of maintaining the status quo, the traditional subject matter, and even the teaching techniques utilized when they were students. The recent graduates are usually strong for innovation and for the incorporation of the newest facets of both subject matter and pedagogy. These two extreme types are heard from as rugged individuals and as members of the alumni association.

A second major group influencing the curriculum, especially in the graduate schools, are the many professional associations. They generally exert pressure for academic reform through the accrediting societies. Closely related to this professional accrediting, and growing in effectiveness, is the work of the regional accrediting bodies, whose efforts are quite helpful.

Another group, usually quite unhelpful, are the non-students. These are the hangers-on and professional protesters who frequent the campus, the library, the coffee shop. They are sometimes students who are, as a rule, against rather than for any reasonable curriculum change. Fortunately they have little effect on the regular academic programs, although in isolated instances, such as Berkeley, they have had considerable effect on co- and extra-curricular activities.

WHAT ARE CO-CURRICULAR ACTIVITIES?

Co-curricular activities are the programs that fall between the regular academic pursuits and the recreationally oriented activities. They are loosely linked to the educational affairs and frequently operated by the institution. Under this category fall such programs as the special lecture series, the chamber music programs, and the artist in residence. They are important to the well-rounded cultural background of all students.

While this portion of the institution's program is usually presented on a voluntary basis, all students should be strongly urged to participate. As in the case of the extra-curricular affairs, such as social events and athletics, the college or university should generously support these activities. Similarly, the faculty should insure that the co-curricular programs are educationally sound, interesting to the students, and related to the philosophy of the institution.

While it may be difficult for many professors to believe, there are some students who are not stupid, hedonistic, or philistine but who nevertheless find the delights of academic analysis, categorization, and discovery rather pale. These students come to college with hopes that are unrealistic, yet legitimate. They wish to learn how to lead a good life. They find, however, that many colleges are not interested in this question. Despite rhetoric about training leaders, even the better colleges are frequently organized on the assumption that the good life is, in fact, the academic life. They offer few experiences outside the classroom, no future except graduate school, and no adult models except scholars. Sometimes this situation can be corrected in a well balanced co-curricular program that approaches intellectual attainment.

WHAT ARE EXTRA-CURRICULAR ACTIVITIES?

These programs are yet another echelon removed from the

purely academic affairs of the institution. Although some students today protest that colleges should be concerned only with developing academic potential, we believe that extra-curricular activities exert a powerful influence on the students participating. Because of the extent of this influence, the faculty should have an interest in them.

These extra-curricular programs, such as inter-collegiate athletics, are conducted by specialists. These instructors, coaches, and directors usually have faculty rank, but are not considered academicians. But, if they have a viable educational philosophy, and if they are experts in their respective fields, they can command the respect and gain the voluntary participation of the students who most need to participate in such activities.

In the early days of American higher education, leadership of extra-curricular activities was obtained from two major sources. The first source, usually used for intercollegiate athletics, was that of former athletes. The second source, usually used for non-physical pursuits, was the faculty members themselves. The latter were broadly gauged individuals who enjoyed participating with students in non-academic pursuits. Debating clubs, musical groups, chess teams, and similar activities are found in this category.

Those who do not see the need for activities such as the preceding overlook the significance of campus living as a living experience itself. As former President Fels of Bennington used to assert, the total college is the teacher. Too frequently we, on college staffs, have had an over-riding concern with the fifteen hours a week the student spends in class, and too little interest in the other ninety-seven waking hours he has at his disposal. The residence hall, the college within the university, even the fraternity house can be important elements in the education of a college student. Perhaps America needs a new kind of college, in which the teachers are not drawn primarily from the academic profession, and the pedagogy does not rely primarily on classrooms.

The continuing professionalizing of some extra-curricular programs, such as intercollegiate athletics, makes it imperative that both faculty and administrators take a greater interest in this important area of student life. Additionally, the social life or student affairs programs of the dormitories or fraternity row are important elements in student growth and development. "It is a very grave error to suppose that the social setting of the school or the class is irrelevant to the learning that goes on. On the contrary, social influences are woven inextricably into the very texture of the learning. They may affect it favorably, or they may affect it unfavorably, but affect it they will."[3]

As greater effort is made to modernize the curriculum and make it more immediately relevant to student needs and desires, a considerable blending of the regular courses with the extra-curricular or co-curricular activities is occurring. Indeed, the efforts of students on campus, and some non-students adjacent to campuses, to have their own thing—their own college—in the way of classes and seminars is, to some extent, influencing faculty members to operate less formally in terms of conducting their classes and laboratory sections. Some colleges and universities have gone so far as to establish related institutions or experimental colleges offering only extra-curricular activities.

WHAT ARE THE MAJOR PROBLEMS IN CURRICULUM?

In addition to the current curricular problems mentioned in earlier sections of this chapter, there are several perennial difficulties that have plagued the academic programs of colleges and universities over the years. These have been examined at length by educational experts, and many remedies have been proposed. Indeed, experimentation has taken place in some of the more progressive institutions, and some headway made in correcting abuses in this area.

It might prove interesting to the reader to observe how these problems have been presented in other studies. On the matter of curriculum design and direction: "The curriculum has received considerable comment herein and elsewhere. As the program of studies, it is the most important activity on campus. And yet, few leaders in higher education completely understand it. Long the province of the faculty, trustees and administrators have largely abdicated responsibility for it as an entity. The result has been obvious. It has become a porkbarrel operation, which because of its uncontrolled proliferation, has been unsound education-ally, has held down faculty salaries, and has frustrated serious students. However the situation may be improving because of the brash suggestion of Beardsley Ruml that the trustees should take over the curriculum. Fortunately, most trustees are too wise for that, but they now realize that someone has to give leader-ship and direction in this vital area. There are indications that trustees, and in some institutions enlightened faculties, are giving greater power to the president primarily for this purpose."[4]

With respect to the origin of the curriculum: "Despite its central place in the program of the college, the curriculum rarely has been made the object of systematic investigation. There is, of course, a vast literature on the curriculum, but most of it was concerned with descriptions of existing programs and with pro-posals for reform rather than with the demonstration of effects upon students. The great curriculum revolutions that have taken place in the United States, such as Eliot's at Harvard, Erskine's at Columbia, Meiklejohn's at Wisconsin or Hutchins' at Chicago, have not been accompanied by controlled observations that would permit comparison, in terms of effects, of one curriculum with another or give evidence that changes in students were due to the curriculum and not to other features of the college environment.

"There have been some efforts to assess scientifically the effects of a particular kind of curriculum—for example, Dressel and Mayhew—and there have been numerous studies of the effects of particular courses. But when scientists have carried on investigations in the colleges, they have tended to stress other aspects of the educational process—aspects such as methods of teaching, the student's sociological background and motivation, and the kinds of associations he forms with his peers. This has been due not alone to the special interests of the investigators but also to the fact that the influence of the curriculum on students has appeared to be much less than the influence of other factors."[5]

With respect to the relationship of various groups on campus to the curriculum: "While the board should formulate policy, it should not implement that policy. On a step-by-step basis, a logical approach to securing optimum academic productivity might be as follows: (1) the educational affairs committee observes the academic programs, (2) it secures the advice of deans or senior faculty members, (3) it reports findings and proposals to the board, (4) the board deliberates on these reports, and (5) with the advice of the president, it formulates policy."[6]

Although we may not agree with all of Ruml's convictions, he is correct in stating that the final decision in any aspect of the institution's operations, including the academic, rests with the trustees: "Trustees do have a legal, overall responsibility that goes much beyond that of the faculties. If the welfare of the college demands it, they should take drastic action—only they have the real power to do it."[7]

The presidents and deans must in the future figure more prominently in curriculum leadership than they have in the past: "The president and certain other administrative officers frequently are qualified by education, training and experience to exert a major influence in the area of the curriculum. Many of these people have been on the faculty, have developed a broad view of the institution's educational needs, and may have more objectivity than some faculty members."[8]

And: "The academic dean must have a close relationship and give guidance to the trustee committees in the instruction sphere. He is the executive officer or administrator closest to the education of students and should have a better grasp of the program than even the president. Unfortunately, many academic deans have neglected to maintain an intimate relationship with faculty members and students. They have become armchair strategists, more concerned with academic bookkeeping than with ideas and people."[9]

And more recently this view: "Since students far more than any other persons are where the educational action is—in the classroom—they are perforce better informed about educational substance and processes. The significance of higher education in the life of the average educated American would doubtless be increased if students sat on committees which determine the character and content of instruction."[10]

While the foregoing comments and quotations indicate a wide range of concerns regarding the curriculum, it seems clear that the most important curriculum problem facing higher education today is who should be in control of the curriculum. Although a number of the previously quoted studies indicated a geniuine need for more participation on the part of the trustees, administrators, and students in curricular matters, we offer the position that no particular individual or specific group has all the answers or should have exclusive dominion in this vitally important and eternally controversial area. We believe that the strong grip that the faculty has had on the curriculum and academic affairs will have to be loosened, the academic administration will have to provide more leadership in this area, and students' needs and desires will have to be given greater consideration in the future than they have received in the past.

DOCUMENTATION AND COMMENTARY

1. Peter F. Drucker, *Managing for Results*, New York: Harper and Row, 1964, xii.

2. A number of colleges and universities have recently completed or are now engaged in self-studies of their academic programs as a first step toward curriculum reform. New York University and Princeton University are just two of these. For a discussion of similar studies at eleven other institutions, the reader is referred to Dwight B. Ladd's *Change in Educational Policy: Self-Studies in Selected Colleges and Universities*, New York: McGraw-Hill Book Company, 1970.

3. James L. Mursell, *Successful Teaching*, New York: McGraw-Hill Company, 1946, 159.

4. Gerald P. Burns, ed., *Administrators in Higher Education*, New York: Harper and Row, 1962, 221.

5. Nevitt Sanford, ed., *The American College*, New York: John Wiley & Sons, Inc., 1962, 418-419.

6. Gerald P. Burns, *Trustees in Higher Education*, New York: Independent College Funds of America, 1966, 90.

7. Beardsley Ruml and Donald Morrison, *Memo to a College Trustee*, New York: McGraw-Hill Company, 1959, 227.

8. Burns, *Trustees in Higher Education*, 91.

9. *Ibid.*

10. Earl J. McGrath, *Should Students Share the Power?* Philadelphia: Temple University Press, 1970, 55.

7 COURSE DETERMINATION

Some years ago at a meeting of the American Council on Education a panel discussion was held featuring statements by Alvin Eurich and Clark Kerr. The issue was innovation in higher education. Dr. Eurich had been in charge of a project which was then coming to its end, and he was reporting to the American Council with considerable chagrin that very little had come out of it. Innovation, in effect, he said, was not being produced by American higher education, and Dr. Kerr supplemented this statement with the flat position that major changes in higher education usually came from external pressures.

WHAT ABOUT COURSE CHANGES?

A major problem in curriculum structure in American higher education, as seen by these experts, is the reluctance of the academic profession to tamper with the status quo. Innovation is badly needed and is greatly feared. Another major problem in the area of course determination is how to figure out some way to get away from the course approach. Not only do educators show reluctance to experiment with their own professional approaches, they demonstrate a grim determination never to be disturbed in ways of doing things that were started during the Renaissance and have changed but little since that time. An example is the fact that much of higher education is transmitted to students via the lecture method. There are few worse types of teaching than the lecture, and yet it is departed from reluctantly, and then only in certain disciplines.

Current practice in the determination of courses involves many people on a campus, and is not limited to administration. Although most courses are suggested by faculty members through their departments on the basis of curricular necessity, students are also now being involved in developing new courses. However, the degree of their involvement varies with the institution and may range from actually suggesting the content for new courses to merely being involved in meetings where new courses are discussed.

In a large public institution, for example, the process may go somewhat like this: a professor gets an idea that a new course is needed, or a group of students suggest such a course to him. He brings the matter up at his department meeting, often with students in attendance, and suggests to his department chairman that the course be introduced in the next catalog. The department chairman appraises the situation, and if he agrees that the course is appropriate, he then puts in a request for it to the dean of the area in which the department is located. If the dean approves, this is sometimes the last step necessary. In some institutions, however, the catalog is often reviewed by a vice-president for academic affairs, or at least by subordinates in his department, before going to the president for final approval.

In a small college the procedure might be considerably simpler and less formal, with the faculty member asking his department chairman for the privilege of introducing a course and the department chairman merely including it in the catalog copy, which then goes before a college-wide curriculum committee for approval.

There are, of course, many variations to this pattern. However, the recent decisions to include students in course development have been very positive steps which not only have tended to make them feel a part of and indeed more responsible for their own education, but have led to an updating of course offerings and the development of many new and relevant courses. Also, the use of academic senates and faculty curriculum committees has injected a new and desirable step into the curriculum process which in some cases results in much tighter and more rigorous screening of new courses than former administrative jurisdiction provided.

It is understandable that only occasionally does an administrator propose a course, and even less occasionally is he successful in having it accepted by the faculty. In one small college the president wished to establish a team-teaching approach at the general education level for the freshman and sophomore years. The course proposed was a history of civilization and involved several disciplines. For several months the faculty valiantly resisted, and then when it became necessary to accede to the president's wishes, the faculty took occasion to structure and restructure the offering every other semester. Within five years the course was a much different creature than it had been at the outset.

ARE RELATED ISSUES INVOLVED?

Once the decision is made to establish a course, however, other decisions must be made as well. How is the course to be structured? This, of course, depends very largely on the faculty member. If he approaches his task scientifically and with an eye to careful planning, he will outline the course, set up goals in terms of amounts of information to be covered, and produce a syllabus for his own guidance, if not for the guidance of his students. Again, if he is a forward thinker, he will set up his reading lists or laboratory experiments or demonstrations, depending on the subject or the disciplines, and schedule these calendarwise so that students know what to expect and when.

The determination of how much credit the course deserves is largely a matter for faculty group decision. In some cases the enthusiast who has proposed the course will consider it to be of greater credit value than colleagues in his department. Usually the number of units to be given for the course will depend on departmental determination, operating within general guidelines established by the institution. An example of such a guideline might be institutional practice of giving one unit for every two hours of laboratory work.

The determination of teaching hours also depends upon faculty decision based upon institutional policy. In public institutions which have rigid rules of behavior laid down by code and law, there is often very little elbow room. One lecture hour counts for so much faculty credit as compared to one laboratory hour. In small or private institutions where arrangements are more flexible, departments and deans often make this decision. A common rule of thumb is that if an instructor spends an hour in front of a lecture class, he gets an hour of teaching credit for it, and if he spends an hour before a demonstration or laboratory class he ordinarily gets less than an hour of teaching credit for it.

There are many problems connected with course determination. Some of these are interesting examples of how faculties can work themselves into very difficult and complex situations.

IS THERE COURSE PROLIFERATION?

One of these problems is course proliferation. Discussed briefly in the previous chapter, this is a disease whose symptoms are evident in every institution of higher education, no matter how large or small. There seems to be an inherent tendency in every graduate student going into college teaching to insist on teaching highly specialized courses in his area of interest. The term *balkanization* has been aptly applied to this tendency, and it results in a chopped-up curriculum of highly specialized, narrow approaches, which, if allowed to develop uncontrolled, departs from educational values and serves only the interests of the researcher in the discipline.

There is a magnificent satire on course proliferation by former Provost J. Harris Purks, Jr., of the University of North Carolina. We quote at some length because it is a classic in its field.

"I doubt that any faculty in formal session would ever generate spontaneously the idea of establishing a curriculum in alligator farm management. The genesis of the development which I shall describe must therefore come either from a faculty member who knows something about alligators, from a dean hell bent on expansion, or from a chief administrator who measures the success of his institution in terms of the number of inches of publicity which it acquires in the national press or from some successful owner or manager of an alligator farm who needs an assistant and thinks that his alma mater can produce one for him.

"Regardless of the source of the idea, the method of development could be essentially as follows: A professor in a department or a school, in a college or university, submits to his department chairman an outline of a course in alligator farm management. The department head perhaps is not enthusiastic at first, but upon being told that the professor can teach the course without additional cost to the institution and after listening to persuasive remarks regarding the need for such a course in the development of the state and region, his half-hearted approval is given. Furthermore he does not want to get the reputation of being an old sour puss. The curriculum committee probably passes it thinking that there will be very little registration anyway, or perhaps the course just appears on the schedule without approval. Checks and balances are not always popular in higher education. It doesn't matter. You see, we all know that some sort of case can be made for anything proposed in the name of education. The responsible head of the institution probably doesn't know about it.

"The professor and probably one or two alligator farm managers, having a community of interests, hold a conference during the summer months. Realizing that there is some strength in numbers, the formation of an association is planned. One of the managers manages to become President of the Association of Alligator Farm Managers; another one of the pioneers becomes Vice President; and another Secretary-Treasurer. Having the officers of the Association established, it now becomes necessary to get members after a few months to prove that the Association exists. Naturally, the Association appreciates the generous and far-sighted action by the institution which provided the course in alligator farm management. But there is one thing that is better than a dish of ice cream. That thing is two dishes of ice cream. The course in alligator farm management as originally given now appears to be merely introductory to the subject. Through the generosity of Amalgamated Fabricators of Alligator Hides, Inc., a fellowship has been established and research work has been done in alligator farm administration. On the basis of this research, an advanced course obviously is needed. Now we have two courses—and eventually three or four. In the advanced course the word *management* is changed to *administration*. Now we have alligator farm administration.

"But the professor in charge of these courses notices that his students do not have sufficient background He finds it necessary to devote a considerable portion of his time in courses to elementary studies of the alligator. Furthermore, he has hopes that he can develop a department of his own. He urges his department head to let him devote his time entirely to alligator farm administration and to bring in an instructor who has read a book on alligators. Total registration in the department has gone up and the head begins to like the idea. Soon we see new courses appearing: (1) The Alligator in the Modern World. The description of this course is interesting. 'The gradual encroachment of man upon the natural habitat of the alligator has injected serious problems and has forced the alligator to retreat further into remote regions. This problem and its impact upon the ratio of free alligators to impounded alligators are covered fully in this course.' (2) The Adolescent Alligator. (3) Orientation to Alligator Farm Administration. (4) Marketing of Hides, and (5) Alligator Skin Products Design. . . .

"It now begins to appear the curriculum still has some gaps. The program has given to the institution a considerable amount of publicity. The institution is the first institution in the nation, perhaps even in the world, to start a curriculum in alligator farm administration. Development must proceed further. Our professor suggests to his department chairman that the next man brought in have a minor in this field. Since the only source of minors is the department itself, a bit of inbreeding starts. Shortly thereafter, other courses appear. (6) Alligator Ecology, the alligator in his environment. (7) The Exceptional Alligator. (8) Exhibitionism in Alligator Farms. (9) Demography, Alligators. . . .

"Having now a reasonably full-blown curriculum and the need for this highly specialized training having been established, the faculty of the institution, after debating the question for a year in exhaustion rather than in enthusiasm, recommends that the course structure constitute a major and that the degree, Bachelor of Science in Alligator Farm Administration, be added to the list of degrees offered by the institution, provided the page is long enough.

"At this point, the responsible head of the institution hears about the matter for the first time. He had, of course, heard rumors that there was an alligator man on the faculty. He might have made inquiry about departmental offerings, but this would likely have been resented as meddling or interfering, or as restriction upon freedom. He is informed that this new degree will not add anything to the institution's budget; after all, the courses and the staff are already present."[1]

Purks goes on with his ludicrous example, explaining how the department becomes a school and how then other institutions, not wishing to be outdone, organize parallel curricula. He explains that considering the limitations upon the professional field, most of the graduates of these departments and schools are turned out for the purpose of teaching in other departments and schools and that a considerable inter-institutional placement business is thus built up. The whole thing is obviously far-fetched, and yet it presents such a frighteningly accurate picture of how many curricula are developed in modern colleges and universities that it warrants our careful attention.

WHAT IS ACADEMIC HOBBY RIDING?

A second problem of course organization and determination, which is related to proliferation and which in fact is one of the causes of it, is professional hobby riding. Almost every graduate student who emerges from an American graduate school starts his teaching job with the idea that research is the only noble profession and that teaching is something one does in order to make money so that he can engage in research. His research specialty, which he has elaborated on in the form of a doctoral dissertation, is ordinarily a very narrow and profound particle of knowledge studied in great depth. The graduate student who has started a teaching career is of the opinion that there is nothing so important as his discipline and in his discipline the most important aspect is the area in which he has chosen to specialize. It is therefore necessary to bequeath to his students such enlightenment as has come to him during his years of graduate study. There are more poor, useless, and futile courses offered every year under such conditions than can be easily numbered.

To sum it up, professional hobby riding is not good for a curriculum, it is not good for a faculty, nor does it contribute to the mission of the institution; yet it, like proliferation, is one of the most difficult problems to control.

WHERE ARE THE CURRENT PRESSURES?

A third problem, which has become ever more evident as institutions of higher education have left their churchly influence and become more and more secular in tone, is the development of courses by faculty members who have certain private political and social goals to pursue. Prime examples of this sort of development are evident in the experimental colleges current at the present time, in which courses in Mao's philosophy, civil disobedience, the relationship of the police to ethnic minorities, and other subjects which have disturbed a good many people become subjects for academic examination.

Many of these topics touch on problem areas in today's

society; the students consider them relevant and are very interested in them. Therefore, if the subjects are really examined academically, this development might be wholly defensible. But, unfortunately on occasion they are not. Some such courses are suggested and established by faculty members who, with the best of intentions, are interested in preaching a sermon or propounding a cause, and they are not valid academic exercises. There is, after all, or there should be at least, something solid, permanent, and eternal in educational approaches to modern problems. To seize upon the changing winds of politics and society as a basis of structuring and restructuring curricula in institutions of higher education is to make academic knowledge a shabby and superficial thing. Obviously current problems must be considered in higher education, but there are ways of considering them in tested and traditional approaches while maintaining appropriate objectivity and scholarly attitudes.

HOW ARE COURSE COSTS DETERMINED?

A fourth problem of course determination is the element of cost. Together with the proliferation of knowledge there has come about a proliferation of educational equipment and facilities. It is no longer merely a matter of a teacher's willingness to devote one hour of his teaching day to a subject. His proposal now may involve computer rental, laboratory equipment of a costly nature, staff work or duplicating machinery, or any one of a number of items which wind up in the institution's budget. The budget is a factor and it must be considered. Ordinarily faculty members do not consider it, and therefore the administration is forced to blue-pencil and to restrain. It would be far better if faculty members developed a realistic view of some of these problems with the idea of sharing some of the responsibility of keeping course offerings within realistic fiscal limits.

WHAT IS THE EDUCATED MAN?

A fifth problem in this area has to do with the rugged individualism of faculty members and administrators as this relates to the definition of an educated man. Pedagogues have been arguing about this for centuries, and only occasionally have approaches been made to an answer. The most recent effective one was the Harvard general education study of the late 1930's which resulted in an epidemic of lower division interdisciplinary courses featuring team-teaching in many colleges and universities of this land. But even in the establishment of such courses there was never any agreement as to what they should contain and never any permanent solution as to their organization. Faculty members simply cannot agree and never have agreed on what constitutes an educated man. The closest thing to an answer that has been provided is a working agreement on the part of faculties that a student should have a sampling of several different disciplines, the sampling to consist of courses supervised and controlled by the disciplines themselves. This is a most inadequate working arrangement, but it is the only one that seems to have any hope of being generally supported by faculties in large numbers.

However, that there is no general agreement on what constitutes a good education should not discourage teachers and professors from constantly trying to come closer to the answer. Currently the tendency seems to be for most people to give up and to allow the various disciplines to offer a cafeteria-style presentation which the student can make the most of through his own initiative.

WHEN DO INNOVATIONS OCCUR?

The sixth and final problem, in connection with the determination of course offerings, is the problem of innovation. Innovation is not popular in higher education, even as it is unpopular in most well-established professions. The professor, it has been said, is perfectly willing to be very liberal with other people's lives and careers, but is completely unwilling to be anything but extremely reactionary with regard to his own. The tendency of American colleges and universities to tie themselves too rigidly to the course-unit-time-credit-hour approach, with complete unwillingness to vary from this pattern, is evidence that very little in the way of genuine innovation has come out of American higher education. True, we have experimented with gadgets, such as educational television, programmed learning, and other devices, but these have never really eroded the stubborn longevity of the course approach.

There are other ways of educating students. For example, it might be interesting to experiment with the idea of having no courses, but only the resources for learning—the people, in the form of faculty, to counsel and advise, and teach in those areas where the Socratic method was necessary or desirable; the books in the library; and the electronic gadgets available for the students' use. In such an experiment an achievement level could be set up in which the student could take examinations when he felt he was ready for them but would no longer be tied to the course-attendance, lecture-listening, credit-hour rut.

This is probably the greatest need in American higher education today—true innovation—the willingness to consider genuinely new approaches to teaching and learning. Although various studies and reports of the last decade coupled with student demands have resulted in some positive changes in curriculum and courses, as long as the conservative American graduate school has a death-grip on the concepts of its students, progress in this area will continue to be slow. This is unfortunate for everyone

and especially for the students themselves, because, as future
faculty members, they transmit this stubborn conservatism to
their own students.

DOCUMENTATION AND COMMENTARY

1. J. Harris Purks, Jr. From an address at the Third State of the University Conference of the University of North Carolina, March 10, 1955.

8 SELECTION PROCEDURES

In obtaining the faculty, the first steps must be to reach agreement upon how the purpose of the institution will be realized. To say the purpose is purely academic is more than a play on words. The purpose or institutional direction is directly dependent upon the curriculum accepted and the courses of study determined. To implement these decisions, the appropriate faculty members must be selected. Any serious consideration of the selection of the faculty in modern higher education must grapple with the problem of who charts the course for the college or the university.

ARE THERE HISTORICAL IMPERATIVES?

In the past ages, higher education's mission was clear, but its techniques were hit-or-miss. Today, however, a complete reversal has occurred. The techniques of higher education have become much more scientific and effective, but higher education's mission is now cloudy and murky to the point of being almost obscured. In the Middle Ages, learning existed to preserve the words of the fathers of the church so that the doctrine of Christianity would not be forgotten. When nationalism superseded the holy Roman empire, higher education became a training ground for a tiny elite devoted to the best interests of the nation in which the institution existed. Thus, the British public schools and universities developed a system of higher education which emphasized classical learning and the concept of the whole man—all aimed, however, at turning out statesmen and leaders who could keep England firmly on her course. In Germany, the role of the professor was even more exalted, and the output of the nation's universities, still concerned only with a tiny elite minority, was destined for military, political, and clerical leadership.

In early America, there was a reversion to the religious emphasis when sect after sect established small church-related colleges built around the commanding figure and personality of a president and designed to carry on the particular traditions of a particular faith. There was no quibbling or arguing in these early, small colleges of America about character development. It was definitely a part of the educational process and it was influenced strongly by sectarianism. In the mid-nineteenth century the federal government began its intrusion into the affairs of higher learning with the Morrill Act which established agricultural and mechanical skills as a proper goal for higher educational institutions. This was truly the beginning of secularism in American higher education, and public universities from that time forward moved farther and farther away from the early religious influence of the small colleges.

WHAT CHANGES IN DIRECTION OCCUR?

Today, secularism has triumphed. The church maintains its influence in only a few of the private institutions of the land, and even in those, its power is waning. West of the Mississippi, the public institutions not only outtalk but also outnumber private institutions of higher education. Even in those strongholds on the east coast where private instiutions are far more numerous than public ones, the William Sloan Coffins consistently remind their colleagues that it is no longer fashionable to be moral according to an institutional code. Today a college or university can tolerate the publication by its students of periodicals containing pornography and obscenity to a degree which a decade ago would have been absolutely unthinkable, and yet this is firmly defended by the advocates and proponents of academic freedom. On the other hand, the singing of Christmas carols is frowned upon in the teacher education departments because this might in some way infringe upon the sensibilities of persons depending upon the first amendment for protection of their emotional calm. The burning of heretics in an auto-da-fé during the Middle Ages was soundly applauded by the intelligentsia of the time. Today, the breaking of the law and the undermining of every existing moral code are similarly applauded by many academics for somewhat the same reasons. At any rate, secularism has triumphed, and whatever ills we now possess are the ills of a society which has firmly separated itself from institutionalized morality.

WHAT ARE THE PURPOSES AND GOALS?

Any contemplation of this development brings up the interesting question—why do we have colleges and universities? For what purpose do they exist?

Obviously, the politicians have an easy answer. The purpose of education, they say, is to prepare people for service to the economy and the state, and to develop their own individual personalities so that they can live full lives. But this is hardly the final purpose of higher education. There must also be involved the search for truth in the development of a new moral code, if the old ones are lacking. There must be some attempt at developing a sense of discrimination among the graduates of large public and private institutions, so that they will be able to tell the difference between good and bad, as well as between right and wrong. There is inevitably some subjectivity involved in determining what the final mission of an institution of higher education should be.

Which brings us, of course, squarely to the question of whether the faculty is qualified to provide all of the guidance required in the solution of this fundamental and basic problem. It seems likely that a scientist would have the college make science the final answer; a humanist would place humanism at the top of the list of institutional priorities; an artist would similarly elevate aesthetics. In fact, the specialist, as a specialist, cannot possibly have the answer. The answer is big and indefinite, and it must be provided by the generalist, the person who has, as a trustee, the mission of the institution under his charge, or as an administrator, the direction of the institution under his control.

IS THERE FACULTY INFLUENCE?

The faculty can and must play a role in the final determination of the mission of the institution. But an institution which is completely dominated by its faculty inevitably falls heir to the problems of academic fragmentation which Clark Kerr attributed to the multiversity. In this case, the bigness, impersonality, and irrelevance encourage the gathering of scholars, each devoted to his own professional ends and goals, where the student is left to enrich his life as best he may, by seizing upon uncoordinated scraps of knowledge as they rush by him in the fast-moving academic production line.

The trustees, not the faculty, should set the mission of the institution. And the trustees should employ administrators who are willing to administer the institution in the light of that mission.

WHAT ABOUT FACULTY SELECTION?

One of the major considerations inevitably associated with the mission of the institution is the problem of who selects the faculty. Obviously, if the institution is moving in the direction of becoming a multiversity with no guidance and no sense of direction, then it makes little difference. Each department can, through its own politicking and pushing, bring about an addition to its numbers of the sort which it approves. Good departments will employ good scholars; mediocre departments, fearful of engendering professional competition, will consistently employ poor scholars; and, the college will proceed on its course in a variety of directions.

We once had an experience with a department of philosophy which had lost its strongest leader, a religion-oriented philosopher who believed firmly in ethics as a fundamental basis of philosophical study. When he died at the height of his career, the department was left with a gaggle of logical positivists and linguistic specialists who were extremely loath to bring anyone else in who might broaden their perspective. The administration did its very best to urge upon them the balancing of their specialties with a man who regarded philosophy as something more than word games, but they would have none of it. The consequence was that that department of philosophy, instead of maintaining its quality as one of the leading departments in its geographic area, became a very narrow group of slanted specialists whose influence on their profession, and, more importantly, on the lives of their students, became small and insignificant.

WHAT ABOUT TEACHING VERSUS RESEARCH?

Another decision that must be made, if the mission of the institution is to be fulfilled, is whether the faculty selection process shall emphasize teaching or research. We have already dealt with this question from other angles, in other parts of this volume, so here it is necessary only to reiterate our earlier position that if teaching is a major goal of the college or university, then men and women must be selected to join the faculty who will respect that goal. We remind the reader again that this is not so easy a thing to achieve as it might seem on the surface, because the American graduate school is busily occupied with turning out people who consider research to be the only appropriate goal of a scholar and who look upon teaching merely as a means of making an inadequate living while engaging in one's chief occupation, that of research.

In many cases, the person who joins the faculty with this approach mellows with the years, soon comes to respect and admire the good teachers around him, and gradually takes on their aspirations as his own. Many scholars become honestly convinced through practice that teaching is far more important than the graduate schools have led them to believe. But the teaching-versus-research controversy is still a serious problem in the selection of faculty, and if the mission of the institution is to be fulfilled, the tendency of American graduate schools to over-emphasize research at the expense of teaching is a problem which must be solved.

HOW IS THE INSTITUTIONAL
MISSION DETERMINED?

What, after all, is the mission of a college or a university? In the university there are really three general missions or major functions—teaching, research, and service. In the small college, chief emphasis is placed on teaching. These major functions occur in every institution and provide the programs in which the specific missions or special emphases are developed. Since the mission grows out of the functions, all the missions are educationally oriented. As such, the educators connected with the college or university—whether they are found on the governing board, in the administration, or on the faculty—must help shape the mission of these institutions.

However, since all colleges and universities exist in and of their communities, be they local, state, regional, or national, and since their board members represent the people of these communities, these trustees and regents, according to both law and tradition, are the determiners of the mission. They make this determination on the basis of their interpretation of what the community needs and desires. They are assisted in making this interpretation by the leaders—political, economic, cultural, and professional—in their areas. Once the institution is established and operating, the administration and faculty begin to exert a modifying influence on the mission.

ARE SELECTION PROCEDURES IMPORTANT?

As the preceding sections of this chapter indicated, careful selection procedures for instructors and professors are prerequisite to fulfilling the mission of the institution as achieved through its curriculum and the various courses therein. The mission or purpose is stated in the charter of the college or university and is attained through its educational program.

The educational program is a result of the offerings or courses taught or directed by the faculty. These offerings, in effect, determine the general direction and aspirations of the institution. Thus, it is imperative that the curriculum, the courses, and the faculty be carefully selected.

All higher institutions are different to some degree. Certainly similar threads run through the fabric of all, but variations predominate. Thus, different academic programs require different people. While a broad spectrum of teachers are sought in the 2,500 American institutions of higher education, the search for them and the methods of selection are similar throughout the profession.

Colleges and universities have different charters and missions because education is as broad as life itself. These institutions differ in the portion of the body of knowledge that they carve out as their offering. Differences occur not only in the areas of knowledge covered, but also in the methods used to present that knowledge.

For example, Harvard College and St. John's College, two of the oldest and most distinguished schools in America, both lay claim to a balanced liberal arts curriculum. But Harvard presents this in traditional fashion (core curriculum plus electives; classes and laboratories), while St. John's uses primarily readings, discussions, and seminars from "The Great Books."

These differences in both the curriculum and the method of presenting it are spelled out in most institutions' catalogs. Thus, these booklets are helpful in the selection process because indirectly they describe and define the type of person needed for a particular assignment at a given institution.

Faculty needs are determined by the division or department head, usually in consultation with the academic dean or provost. The actual selection of the new person is made in various ways, depending upon the traditions of the institution and the importance of the position. In some instances, the president and/or dean is involved, but usually the candidates are screened by a small departmental committee, and the choice is made by the chairman when a concensus is achieved.

With increasing frequency, search committees are becoming concerned with qualifications of candidates other than their proficiency in their subject field. Selection in the days ahead will concern itself with such matters as interest and skill in teaching, ability to work effectively with students as demonstrated by personality and temperament, and a broader level of what might be called common sense. We strongly believe that the faculty member of the future is going to be judged more critically by his peers, his superiors, and his students. In addition to knowing his discipline, he will have to know how best to present it. Stress will be placed upon communications, personal relations, and the ability to work as a member of a team within a department or division, within a college or university. The concept of the faculty member's being at the core of a community of scholars and interacting with other members of that community, be they students or administrators, is being revived, analyzed, and adopted. Thus, selection procedures are assuming some new dimensions that all responsible for this activity must comprehend.

9 RECRUITMENT PROCEDURES

Today the college job market is going through a dramatic and complete reversal of form. Whereas only a few short years ago there were far more college positions open than there were qualified candidates to fill them, today there is an over-abundance of well qualified Ph.D.'s looking for work. This places colleges in the advantageous position of being in a buyer's market.

WHAT ARE THE CURRENT FACTORS INFLUENCING FACULTY RECRUITMENT?

Higher education has experienced a period of rapid growth and expansion during the past three decades. The number of college-age students in our population has increased steadily as has the percentage of this group continuing their education after graduation. Thus campuses have expanded, new facilities have been built, and new faculty have been hired to meet the needs of this swelling student population. However, this rapid growth pattern has changed, and even with the potential increase in college student population which open admissions offer, colleges and universities are now in a position to accommodate all those students who desire a college education and who deserve to be admitted. As Allan M. Cartter, former Chancellor of New York University and one of the first to predict the trend, reported, "The percentage of high school graduates who enter some type of formal post-secondary school education was close to 25 per cent in 1940; by 1960 it had risen to 55 per cent, and today it is about 70 per cent. Graduating high school seniors are now about 82 per cent of the 18-year-olds, and a sizable fraction of them graduate only by virtue of serving out their time. Thus we have nearly exhausted rising college entry percentages as a service of expansion."[1]

What this reversal in the growth pattern now means for those seeking employment as college teachers is clear. Again, according to Cartter, "At the peak of (higher education) expansion, 1964 and 1965, we hired five teachers for every one that died or retired—that is one as a replacement and four to meet growing enrollments. For the 1970-77 period this ratio will probably drop to 3:1; in the 1978-85 period it promises to be less than 2:1. The decrease in demand for college teachers is almost as dramatic in absolute terms. In 1964-65 we needed about 18,000 new college teachers just to meet expanding enrollments; for the next few years this will average about 12,000, and in all likelihood, it will decline to about 7,500 annually a decade from now."[2]

This rapid turn in the job market has created many problems not the least of which is that many individuals are hired who are over qualified and in many instances thus unqualified for the positions they fill. An example of this is the large number of Ph.D.'s being hired to teach in community colleges where they are neither qualified by interest nor training to perform the tasks they are doing or to work with the type of student they meet there.

HOW ARE FACULTY RECRUITED?

However, now that colleges face a buyer's market does not mean they should stop actively recruiting and wait for individuals to come to them. Indeed, during this period when so many well-qualified people are seeking employment may be just the time for colleges to improve the quality if not the quantity of their faculties. Faculty members are recruited through a variety of processes and the college still interested in attracting the best possible candidates is encouraged to continue using all of them just as if the job market were reversed.

One of the most common methods of recruitment is to have faculty members themselves, or department chairmen, or deans, or presidents attend the annual meetings of various professional and educational associations and make use of the professional slave markets that exist in each of these gatherings. This can be a fairly effective way of finding competent people, but in today's tight job market it also exposes the recruiter to the blandishments of many individuals who have found jobs hard to get, and he must be careful not to have his time wasted by individuals of this sort. However, the annual meeting, the convention, and the conference are all effective places for locating recruits.

A second method is to contact colleges or universities with graduate schools which are turning out individuals in fields useful to the institution in question. In some cases, department chairmen are the ones contacted, and this is probably the most reliable method of getting competent recommendations. In others, the institutional placement office will set up a series of interviews. Here again, the danger is that less well-qualified individuals, or those who are not strongly recommended by their own major professors, may occupy much of the recruiter's time.

Correspondence is another method of rounding up a list of usable names. Writing to people one knows in certain fields, or to the national officers of educational associations or professional associations which have a good many professional contacts, is also an effective means of producing recruits. Correspondence moves in both directions, so the letter of application, unsolicited, must also be considered. These, however, must be regarded carefully because the qualifications of the writers may vary widely.

One final word on the matter of recruitment is to remind universities that their recruiting, for both academic and non-academic positions, should be carried out in a manner so as to satisfy the *Higher Education Guidelines* of the Department of Health, Education and Welfare. This means they should seek out qualified women and members of minority groups as actively as they have recruited white males in the past. Such a search not only should include the traditional approaches mentioned above but may also include looking in some areas previously unexplored. For example, universities may want to consider for employment faculty members now teaching at predominantly women's colleges and predominantly minority colleges as well as seeking qualified minorities or women currently employed in non-academic positions.

ARE THERE STEPS IN THE RECRUITMENT PROCESS?

First, a broad screening base should be established. That is to say, as long a list of names as possible should be acquired.

Second, each person named should provide the institution with a *vita*, a list of references, a bibliography of professional publications, if such exists, and a dossier of as much professional and educational information about the individual as is available.

Third, there should be some attempt at a personal interview. In the case of an institution with a low budget, this may mean having an institutional representative make a circuit tour to interview several candidates. A more desirable method is to have the candidate come to visit the institution, meet its people —including student representatives—, and survey in person what is offered.

Fourth, the final and perhaps the most important step in the recruiting process is to engage in an in-depth investigation of those few candidates who are most qualified. This means going to persons not on the candidate's reference list who were associated with him in earlier academic or professional responsibilities and deriving all of the information possible from this search.

Fifth, after the recruiting investigation is completed, then the task is to sign the person up. Given the current market condition, colleges should be at an advantage in this stage of the process, for the number of institutions attempting to lure any one candidate will be significantly fewer than in previous years.

However, a candidate expects certain specific things in the position he accepts. He expects a reasonable and competitive salary arrangement which is basic to his willingness to accept a position. In addition, he wants and expects a certain range of fringe benefits, including such items as the possibility of reasonably periodic sabbaticals, research assistants, insurance programs, and possibly tuition exchange arrangements for his children if the institution is a private one. He may also seek housing, a possibility of cut-rate loans, and as many of the others items which colleges and universities have hit upon to attract and retain faculties in recent years as he can possibly obtain. He also wants a reasonable teaching load.

The candidate also expects something firm and definite in writing, preferably a contract which spells out the conditions of his probationary period, roughly how long it might last, and what his expectations may be in connection with his first year of work. In some state institutions even this relatively simple process has been complicated by the fact that the legislature delays acting on the salary budget until late spring or early summer. This makes a firm contract impossible until long after the recruitment period is over. In such cases, every effort should be made to have special arrangements provided by the legislature so that at least a firm understanding can be made with faculty recruits along about December, January, or February. If this is impossible, the wording of the letter must be such as to leave open the possibility of a change in the legislature's attitude, but should provide maximum encouragement, so that the candidate will not feel that he is signing up for something highly tentative —which usually is not the case.

WHO IS RESPONSIBLE FOR RECRUITMENT?

The focusing of responsibility for the recruitment process is a most important item which is casually ignored by many colleges and universities. It is essential to have the legal responsibility for the contract letter placed in someone's hands and to have that assignment clearly understood by everyone on the campus, so that letters of understanding, which may turn out in court to constitute legal contracts, will not be loosely written. Sometimes department members even with the best of intentions find themselves in the position of having committed the institution inadvertently. In a small college, of course, the place for this responsibility is on the president's desk. In a larger one, it probably belongs with the vice president for academic affairs or the dean of the faculty. In some cases, where the divisions of the university operate with a great deal of autonomy, deans of particular schools exercise this responsibility. Wherever it is, it should be vested in a single individual in the operating unit, and his responsibilities should be thoroughly understood and accepted by all of his colleagues.

ARE THERE ALTERNATIVE APPROACHES?

One comment might be made about the two general approaches to recruitment. One of these is the professional approach, which is carried on by word of mouth, hearsay, scholarly communication, contacts at professional meetings, and similar relationships. The other is the job placement–advertising–employee recruitment process which might or might not make use of a professional agency, printed advertising, or institutional placement offices. Although the dearth of faculty openings is significantly increasing the number of job seekers using the latter, in a professional field such as higher education, the former usually turns up the best people. Generally speaking, agencies are more applicable to jobs rather than professional positions, and even though many enterprising employment agencies are turning their attention and abilities to the needs of the professional man, they are seldom successful in replacing the less formal but nevertheless highly practical system of professional contact, communications, and meetings. What we are saying is that it is perfectly all right to use formal placement services as such, but it is doubtful if the best candidates will be produced by them.

DOCUMENTATION AND COMMENTARY

1. Allan M. Cartter, "Faculty Manpower Planning," in G. Kerry Smith, ed., *The Troubled Campus, Current Issues in Higher Education 1970*, San Francisco: Jossey-Bass, Inc., Publishers, 1970, 233.

2. *Ibid.*, 234-235.

10 ORIENTATION PROCEDURES

The previous chapters have indicated that we feel faculty members need and deserve more and better orientation to their assignments. This pointing of direction or suggesting the approach to the attainment of institutional and professional goals can and should take place when the new faculty member is hired and throughout the career of all faculty and administrators while employed by the institution.

WHAT IS FACULTY ORIENTATION?

It is the exposure of the teachers to various kinds of programs which will enable them to achieve greater success and satisfaction in their work at the institution. By exposure is meant participation and involvement. The kinds of programs are roughly divided into four groups—subject matter, teaching techniques, institutional traditions, and professional relationships. The success and satisfaction sought is both personal and professional. While these relate primarily to his assignment at his institution, broad-based orientation has a spill-over that transcends the immediate assignment and makes a contribution relating to higher education generally.

It is the conviction of the authors that one of the great weaknesses in higher education is the absence of sound programs of faculty orientation. Many of the problems faced by faculty on campus could be temporarily minimized, if not solved completely, if instructors and professors had the benefit of intensive and extensive introduction to their subject, department, and college opportunities and responsibilities.

Many institutions publish faculty manuals designed to present information of interest and importance to new instructors. However, these cover chiefly the rules and regulations of the college. Institutional tradition, academic philosophy, and professional relationships are seldom presented in these publications. Even when and where comprehensive manuals are available, they are poor substitutes for face-to-face discussion.

WHY IS ORIENTATION IMPORTANT?

It is important that all faculty members be involved in some institutional in-service education because all need it at one time or another. Not only should it prove helpful personally and professionally to the recipients, but it will undoubtedly make their contribution more meaningful to the institution.

Faculty members coming into a department for the first time cannot expect to understand all the nuances of their relationships to their colleagues, their students, and their institution from merely reading the catalog. Whether fresh from graduate school or coming from another college, they need an introduction to the institutional policies, both written and unwritten, under which they will be working. Since their internal assignment also has a bearing on their external or their professional status, they should understand what expectations will be made in this area as well.

Faculty members who are old-timers will find orientation sessions important in terms of providing a review of the above considerations, but more particularly for other reasons. There is a tendency on the part of all professional people to get set in their ways. Professors and administrators can utilize information gleaned from departmental discussions of new substantive discoveries and institutional dialogue dealing with innovations in pedagogy. Those who are most distinguished realize that all the areas of man's knowledge are expanding with such rapidity that few can remain posted on everything; that even the learned journals and professional conferences leave much to be covered; that the give and take of institutional seminars are highly valuable. Moreover, they also recognize that the art of communication and the science of teaching are undergoing methodological revolutions; that enlightened teachers must employ the most effective means of stimulating thought; that those using the newest devices will be the most successful.

Stated another way, there are three good reasons why the faculty of the future will insist on adequate briefing sessions. First, the well-oriented teacher is more *productive* in the classroom and laboratory. He knows his subject matter, and he understands how to present it most effectively. Second, the well-oriented teacher *comprehends* the personal and professional relationships in which he is involved. He is sympathetic to the problems of his students, his colleagues, and the other related groups on and off campus. Third, the well-oriented teacher is *inspired* to do the kind of superior job that proves most satisfying to him by insuring his professional success. He takes pride in his teaching, his institution, and his profession.

WHAT ARE THE AIMS AND OBJECTIVES OF ORIENTATION?

The aims or objectives of faculty orientation are slightly different for the young instructor as opposed to the tenured professor. For the former, they embrace the notion long used in industry that an adequate introduction to a new organization pays rich dividends. The neophyte should have careful presentations of the nature and reasons for such esoteric things as institutional traditions and professional relationships. His orientation should include a review of such subject matter coverage and teaching techniques as his department chairman feels is necessary. But, since it may be assumed that he has a solid grasp of his discipline—at least his area of specialization within it—and has had some exposure to the best methods of presenting it, the idiosyncrasies of the institution and the politics of the profession should receive greatest emphasis.

The aims and objectives of orientation for the experienced faculty member should be to acquaint him with additions to his subject matter and inform him of new techniques of presenting his material. This is a sensitive subject with the older professors, and yet they are the ones who can profit most from such orientation. It is with this group that subtle persuasion must be used to bring them, not force them, into the sessions which in many cases they require more than the younger teachers.

The overall objective for all faculty members, as implied above, is to give them the kind of help that will increase their professional productivity within the institution. A secondary aim is to give them a feeling of success and satisfaction in their chosen work. A third is to move them ahead in assimilating new knowledge about their own disciplines.

WHAT ARE THE GOALS OF ORIENTATION?

The goals of orientation are (1) to improve the individual performance, (2) to provide better teaching for and learning by the students, and (3) to enhance the entire educational program of the institution.

These goals are presently being achieved, at least in part, by those hundreds of colleges and universities currently conducting regular programs of in-service seminars for their faculty. But, until all higher institutions embrace orientation in some form, the problem of inadequate perspectives and unfulfilled responsibilities will remain to plague us.

One goal deserving of special mention is that of continuing the valued traditions of the institution. Private colleges in particular should make an earnest effort to maintain those features or characteristics that set them apart from others. One of the great assets of the independent institution is its individuality. The history and happenings that insure its difference should be fully presented to and perpetuated among faculty members, especially new faculty members.

Another goal worth achieving, particularly in the orientation of senior members of the faculty, is that of recognizing desirable relationships with other institutions. All colleges and universities are hard pressed for money, and considerable savings can be made (and possibly transferred to faculty salaries) if various institutions in close proximity geographically or scholastically will work more closely together. This kind of togetherness and the reasons for it are best achieved and understood when fully discussed through regular programs of orientation.

In years past, such orientation as was given was designed primarily for the new staff member. Few, if any institutions, carried on an in-service program for faculty beyond the initial or probationary period. Now, however, there are indications of a definite trend toward a kind of continuous orientation for all members of the staff, faculty, administration, and sometimes trustees. If the contention is correct, that education is an ever-changing endeavor, then certainly we all need continuous professional refreshment. John Gardner's essays on excellence and

the need for constant spiritual, emotional, and intellectual refurbishment emphasize the value of such orientation. As knowledge in our subject fields expands exponentially and as our
institutions become larger and more complex, it is logical to
assume that we need and deserve continuous updating on both
facets.

WHO CONDUCTS THIS PROGRAM?

Orientation programs are conducted by various kinds of people, depending upon the subject under discussion and the avail-
ability of leadership.

At the departmental level where new dimensions of disciplines
are under analysis, the chairman or some senior experts in the
subject should lead the session. If the discussion turns to innovations in teaching techniques, to the motivation of learning, or
to student guidance, then outside specialists have much to contribute.

At the college level where the traditions and policies of the
institution are being presented, the president or the dean is
probably best qualified to provide leadership. If the discussion
deals with professional relationships, either within a discipline
or in higher education generally, an independent consultant is
usually brought in.

The responsibility for leadership in orientation should reside
in the executive officer of the particular unit involved, just as in
the case of regular faculty meetings. In the case of a university,
it should be the president or provost; in a college, the president
or dean; in a division or department, the dean or department
head. Addressing this point, Henderson succinctly observes that,
"The deans of colleges could be more helpful than they commonly are in the exercise of this function."[1]

WHERE AND WHEN DOES
ORIENTATION OCCUR?

This kind of special education for faculty should take place within the institution. It should occur at regular intervals, or at least at the beginning of each academic year.

Faculty meetings are usually held in a hall or large room where all can be accommodated. On the other hand, *faculty orientation* sessions are most effective if held in small groups in a comfortable room. Since there is a closer community of interest within departments, most successful orientation sessions are held in or close to the chairman's office. Many institutions have found it expedient to have occasional sessions off campus at a relaxing resort or in the home of the chairman.

Timing of orientation sessions is especially important for the newly arrived instructor. It is erroneous to assume that incoming faculty members who have briefly visited the campus for one or two interviews can comprehend such esoteric matters as the traditions of the college or such concrete matters as the policies of the institution. Thus, their introductions to these and other important items should occur early in the academic year.

Most colleges now offer at least a full day for freshman orientation. Incoming students are bewildered and need some gentle handling and careful explanation of what's going on. Frequently these student sessions cover a longer period and are devised for recreation as well as education. Reed College has the pleasant tradition of a freshman orientation for a full weekend on nearby majestic Mt. Hood. These sessions usually precede registration and the start of classes.

There is every reason to believe that faculty members can profit from similar treatment. For new faculty it should be pro-

vided before school opens. There are some sound arguments for
holding the sessions on campus and including a tour of the
physical plant as part of the orientation program.

WHY HAVE ANY ORIENTATION?

It is incumbent on professional people that they understand
fully their responsibilities and continue to grow in their area of
specialization. Scholars and educators are no exception to this
rule. Indeed their obligations to their profession and to their
institutions make it imperative that they initially, and throughout their tenure, receive adequate orientation.

One of the great criticisms of higher education today is that
faculty members do not have a clear impression of precisely
what their role should be in certain institutions and under particular situations. For example, if instructors and professors were
properly introduced to the functions and purposes of administration and organization they would not seek to participate so
extensively in these non-teaching pursuits.

On this subject Henderson notes that, "Policy determination
or the formation of broad outlines of curriculum or the formulation of criteria for student achievement may be clearly within
the province of the faculty as a group. On the other hand, the
administration has a definite role in implementing the policies.
Faculty bodies, feeling very protective about their prerogatives
in academic matters, have a strong tendency to want to engage
in administrative detail. Thus they create a vast array of committees, of which the chairman of each becomes a sort of administrative officer, and they clutter up the work of these committees
with extensive matters of detail. As a result the faculty members
become greatly overburdened with routine and a significant
portion of their time is consumed in discussions where a group
of ill-informed and ill-prepared professional men and women

are attempting to give a united opinion on matters that are essentially ones of administrative efficiency."[2]

WHAT IS GENERAL VERSUS SPECIFIC ORIENTATION?

General orientation deals with those matters of interest to all faculty members. These are chiefly institutional, such as: college organization; faculty policies, meetings, and committees; individual responsibilities; facilities for faculty; payroll and financial matters; academic regulations; and the student personnel program.

Other forms of general orientation include the treatment of teaching techniques. Henderson suggests that, "College teaching deserves to be improved. Few faculty are definitely superior as teachers, a substantial portion of them could make considerable improvement, and the remainder badly need to make such an effort. The solution to the problem requires administrative leadership of the most diplomatic and persuasive kind."[3]

Although a poor teacher cannot be made a great teacher merely by exposure to a few sessions of pedagogy, the level of effectiveness can be raised if the master teacher inspires and educates the beginner to perform more efficiently. Henderson again scores strongly in suggesting, "Unfortunately, a principal stumbling block in the way of progress is the failure of the college teachers themselves to examine the subject critically and objectively. They seem content with the timeworn statement that to be a good teacher one needs to know his subject thoroughly and that is it. Indeed it is not uncommon to find prevailing within a department or a faculty an attitude approaching scorn toward the subject of educational methods. This attitude is passed down from generation to generation.

"Is it not reasonable to suppose that half or more of any

faculty could increase the effectiveness of their teaching by developing a clear understanding of the teaching-learning process, and by special attention to the planning of their courses and to their methods of teaching?"[4]

Specific orientation deals with those areas of interest to various segments of the faculty. These include subject matter considerations and special methods for presenting particular material. These will differ in the various divisions and sometimes even within the departments. Although orientation to the various disciplines is primarily the function of the learned society or professional association in that particular academic field, many institutions are including such material in their on-campus sessions.

The point was made in an earlier chapter that college deans, department chairmen, and other senior people in the academic side of higher institutions should play a more active role in advising and assisting—some use the bad word *supervising*—their younger colleagues. The reason for such activity is to improve the performance of the younger men. This can be accomplished in other ways as well. For example, in a recent personal letter to the authors, Dr. William P. Fidler, the nationally known and widely respected former General Secretary of the American Association of University Professors suggests that, ". . . each relatively inexperienced probationary teacher should have a senior member of the department assigned to him for full-scale guidance—classroom visitations, advice on teaching methods and testing, guidance in all phases of professional adjustment, and father confessor on things in general. I would hope that this experienced adviser would be frank with the probationer in all respects, especially where advance criticism appears to be needed, but the adviser might appropriately make a confidential report to the departmental chairman at intervals. The probationer should feel free to request a different adviser if serious differences arise. If higher education does not soon inaugurate such a system, the activists in our midst will probably succeed in getting a rigid grievance machinery established which could very well lessen professional standards rather than improve them. Already we hear demands that *reasons* must be given for non-reappointments, and that the affected teacher should have the right to contest these reasons in a hearing. With thousands of non-renewals a year—most of which apparently do not compromise sound practices (to judge by the small number of complaints from probationers)— required grievance hearings on all non-reappointments would be costly on most counts, and in my judgment unnecessary if workable *orientation and guidance* are established generally."[5]

HOW DOES IN-SERVICE TRAINING OPERATE AS ORIENTATION?

Industrial and governmental organizations desirous of instructing or inspiring their personnel have for the last century offered what is called in-service training. Sometimes this is termed on-the-job education, because this is an apt description of it.

Educational organizations have been slow to accept and incorporate this as a regular adjunct of their programs. Administrators and faculty members felt that colleges and universities, as educational institutions, had no need to train their own teachers. Indeed, the very word *training* was thought to have a connotation *infra dig.* of the professionals on the staff of a higher institution.

In consequence of this, few colleges and universities had more than get-acquainted sessions—usually at the first faculty meeting of the academic year—until recently. Since one of the drawbacks to such desirable programs was the nomenclature, those in the vanguard changed the title to faculty orientation.

Whether called in-service training or faculty orientation, the program was, is, or should be much the same. It is an educational program for teachers, currently employed by the institution, designed to increase their understanding and thus enhance their effectiveness.

Orientation programs extant vary in time from one hour to two days; content varies from a consideration of institutional policies to national professional policies; the leadership varies from the president, dean, and senior faculty members to visiting experts; the place varies from a faculty meeting room to a resort hotel.

HOW CAN ORIENTATION BE IMPROVED?

Every institution of higher education should have an adequate program of faculty orientation. Those that have one should make certain that it fulfills their needs in terms of providing both special or institutional and general or professional information and guidance. Most programs extant could be improved if the president, dean, division heads, or department chairmen gave careful consideration to this important aspect of their faculty leadership. Among the items that should be examined to bring about such improvement are the following: the organization of the sessions, including such matters as the date, time, regularity and frequency of meetings; the administration of the sessions, including such matters as the leadership, place of meeting, method of presentation, and attendance requirement; the content of the sessions, including a broad spectrum varying from institutional regulations and college traditions to innovative teaching techniques and new subject matter in particular disciplines.

IS THERE ANY NEGATIVE ORIENTATION?

Unfortunately there are some adverse aspects of faculty orientation. These usually occur by accident rather than design. Persons in charge of such in-service education of teachers and administrators should guard against negative discussions that militate against the institution or the profession.

Faculty pressure groups, usually small but highly vocal minorities, have a tendency to seize upon any meeting to inflict their questionable leadership on the large but usually inactive faculty as a body. Labor union approaches should be recognized for what they are and should be kept out of orientation dialogue.

Certain administrators have been accused of attempting to influence if not brainwash faculty members toward certain lines of action thought by the American Association of University Professors to be inimical to academic productivity. Since the other two groups on campus, students and trustees, are seldom involved in either faculty meetings or faculty orientation, they are seldom suspect in this area.

A word of caution should be injected at this point. Experience at several institutions has proven that it is better to forego orientation than to attempt to provide it under anything but the best conditions. In this instance, half a loaf is not so good as none! Rather than present to a busy and brilliant faculty an in-service or information program that is not well conceived or properly executed, it is better to hold off on any effort until the optimum conditions are at hand. The subject matter of the orientation program, the timing of the program, and the presenters of the program should be right in the context of the institution.

DOCUMENTATION AND COMMENTARY

1. Algo D. Henderson, *Policies and Practices in Higher Education,* New York: Harper and Brothers, 1960, 188.
2. *Ibid.,* 240.
3. *Ibid.,* 176.
4. *Ibid.,* 177.
5. Letter from Dr. William P. Fidler, former General Secretary of the American Association of University Professors, n.d.

SECTION THREE

Problems of the
Faculty

INTRODUCTION TO SECTION THREE

Just as Section Two of this book dealt with the five primary aspects of building the faculty, this section deals with the six major activities that are considered problem areas to and by the faculties of higher institutions. Undoubtedly there are other similar areas deserving of exploration, but these offer sufficient latitude in terms of possible controversy and conflict to warrant investigation and discussion in the light of current concerns.

We refer to these as problem areas in the generic sense of that term; we say that in these six areas exist the seeds of controversy and conflict; thus, we recognize that these topics present difficulties to trustees, administrators, and faculty alike; we have chosen them for comment in this final section of the book precisely because they defy easy answers.

Having discussed the basic functions of faculty at the beginning of the volume, and having explored the building of the faculty in the center of the volume, we feel it is appropriate to suggest quite candidly some solutions to the perennial dilemmas of relationships and unions, retention, remuneration, promotion, sabbaticals, and ethics in the concluding chapters.

As in the case of two earlier sections, it is unlikely that all educators will agree with our comments in this final section. Indeed, as collaborators in this analysis, even the three of us sometimes blinked when eyeball to eyeball on a few of these issues.

However, we offer our consensus of opinion based upon both personal experience and the millenium of wisdom of colleagues interrogated and authors quoted. We hope this consolidation of thought and observation will prove helpful, or at least stimulating, in advancing the cause of higher education.

ADMINISTRATIVE
11 RELATIONSHIPS
AND UNIONS

A western professor-author writing in a publication devoted to the interests of a union-type faculty organization has made an extended case for delegation of authority to the faculty. There is, he said in effect, little use in perpetuating the fiction of administrative leadership in academic policy because faculty members actually have control over it now and could render adverse administrative decisions ineffective by simply refusing to cooperate. As for the old theory of equating authority and accountability, he said, this simply did not apply in his view to an academic organization, because the faculty was the only possible source of leadership, initiative, and originality.[1]

These are arguments which sound pleasant to many professors, and they are gaining wider and wider circulation as there develops in this nation a drive on the part of certain faculty leaders for administrative authority of a sort which they have never before requested or demanded. The question is whether such concepts are reasonable and workable or, in fact, militate against the faculties' true influence and responsibility in their appropriate areas of academic development and professional evaluation.

WHAT IS THE ROLE OF FACULTY IN ADMINISTRATION?

What is the true and appropriate role of faculty in administration? How much should faculty members administer the institution? To what extent should they involve themselves in administrative decisions? If students are given a role in institutional decision making, what should the faculty role be in relation to that? Should authority be delegated to faculty? If so, how much, and what should it be? These are vital questions and are deserving of straight answers throughout the United States. From coast to coast, these questions are being asked with greater or lesser emphasis in most colleges and universities. Let us first set down several basic concepts which must be included in an intelligent discussion of this subject.

The first concept is that times change, and we are currently facing a unique development of higher education which alters some of the ground rules in faculty-administration relationships. Not many decades ago, most college and university faculties were true communities of scholars, small enough to be dealt with in person by deans, presidents, and chancellors. The institutional environments were small enough so that the pressures of internal organizational politics did not generally apply. It was one thing thirty or forty years ago for a president to go to his faculty, inform them of the amount of money he thought would be available for salary increases, and explain to them the basis of his impending proposal. It is quite another thing for a president today to propose salary increases with a background of screaming newspaper headlines of faculty protest against impossible working conditions, petitions requesting union representation being signed by employee associations and other interest groups, and declarations by legislators in response to this pressure that certain steps should or should not be taken. Traditions have changed radically, particularly in public institutional management.

The second concept is the need for full faculty participation in the formulation of academic policy. Great institutions have built their greatness on the sound professional counsel of faculty groups. Administrators beset with perplexing problems can often get excellent advice from faculty colleagues. The usefulness of the institution can be maintained best by keeping up-to-date through the current research of faculty members in many fields. As a professional group, faculty members are far better qualified to deal with infractions of their own professional code than any outsider—if they are willing to undertake the responsibility. The standards of the institution and its demand level are often more rigorous and appropriate when set by faculty members than when set by administrators who have many conflicting problems to solve, including such things as student enrollment, tuition increases, and political pressure. The faculties' professional participation in the formulation of many types of institutional policy and direction is standard procedure in most colleges and universities.

AT WHAT POINTS DO MANAGERS
AND TEACHERS INTERACT?

A third area concerns the particular roles of faculty and administration, and acceptance of the concept that both are essential in the policy-making process. The professor, in essence, is a specialist and, as such, should bring the specialist's concerns to the policy-making procedure. The president, in essence, is a generalist and brings the generalist's concerns to the policy-making procedure. Neither influence can be overwhelming, or the institution suffers. If the generalist prevails, the result is often a mediocre institution in which the specialist's desires for high quality and high standards run a poor second to overall institutional concerns. If the specialist prevails, as he has in recent years in large research-oriented universities, then the institution ceases to be a true university and, in the words of Robert Hutchins, becomes only a collection of specialists devoted to nothing more than their own interests, and the student and the mission of the institution both suffer. The multiversity as defined by Clark Kerr is a good example of this type of development.

WHAT ARE THE CHARACTERISTICS
OF ADMINISTRATORS?

A fourth concept is that a different type of person will be required for academic administration in the higher education institution of the future. In the past it has been generally conceded that the best college president was a person who came out of the classroom with chalk dust on his coat, who could understand and appreciate the peculiar and unique attributes of the college and university faculty, and who by that fact could get most out of them in terms of professional contributions to the institution. Today, however, higher education has become such big business that management techniques of the highest caliber must be applied, and this requires a different type of person from that ordinarily associated with academics. It may well be that the systems research corporations or industries which regularly employ many Ph.D.'s have set the pattern for the best type of academic management for colleges and universities in the future.

A final concept is that the administration exists to fulfill several roles. It must act as an expediter for the faculty to insure that professors are paid well enough so that morale is reasonably good; to provide the facilities and equipment so that the faculty can do its best work; and—not least important—to help the faculty create an appropriate and beneficial professional environment. The administrator cannot create a professional environment by himself. This must be done by the faculty, but he can aid and assist the faculty in so doing. The administration provides leadership and perspective in terms of facing up to existing problems and foreseeing future problems which the specialist with his narrow view simply does not perceive.

Finally, there is the problem of the administrator seeing to it that the college or university fulfills its mission as laid out by its governing board.

WHAT IS THE CURRENT SIGNIFICANCE OF FACULTY IN ADMINISTRATION?

As has been pointed out, faculty members in most reputable colleges and universities in the United States today already play a significant role in policy making and in administration. In most of the better institutions, the appointment and recruitment of new faculty are left largely to the department. The candidate's future colleagues select him and judge his qualifications. In most instances, faculty members recommend on the granting of tenure and on promotion. The final decisions on these matters are usually left to deans or presidents, but most of the process is under the control of the faculty and any variance from the faculty's recommendation is serious enough to create a major issue.

The faculty also has much to say in most colleges and universities about curriculum and program. Requirements for degrees are proposed by the faculties; courses are set up and administered by the faculty. There are few aspects of curriculum development, except as they relate to the broad and basic mission as a whole, of which the faculty members are not almost fully

in control. Indeed, it is because of this very significant role in
the above and similar decisions that we believe faculty members
are already a part of higher education management rather than
employees, as is suggested by those advocating faculty unions
as a means of getting more power for the faculty.

Relationships between faculties and administrations are generally satisfactory throughout the nation and can be counted on
to produce benefits which are mutual and continuing. However,
problems sometimes occur. Just as eternal vigilance is the price
of individual liberty, so also is it the price of an effective working
relationship between these two types of professionals who are
both in their own way devoted to the best interests of higher
education.

This is not a situation in which faculties are yearning for
authority and responsibility which has yet to be granted. Many
fundamental changes of importance have been made in institutional organization so that their aspirations can be realized.
Quite properly, faculty members are already in control of many
aspects of higher education. In some institutions the only remain-
ing prerogatives of administration are those of acting as an inter-
mediary with the governing board, retaining the veto power in
the case of certain major decisions relating to curriculum and
personnel, and controlling the budget. Even these are being
increasingly influenced by departmental recommendations in the
larger institutions.

ARE THERE PROBLEMS OF FACULTY-
ADMINISTRATION RELATIONSHIPS?

One problem is the desire of faculty to select the administrators. In most colleges and universities with any venerability,
faculty members, and students as well, play a role in this process.
In some cases it is not an important one, and in others it is

considerable. But the concept that an administrator should be appointed in a way which makes him responsible to the faculty rather than to the board of trustees is fallacious. Experience has proven that such appointments will not react to the benefit of the total institution. The mission of the institution is the responsibility of the board of control, and it is up to the president to see to it that that mission is carried out.

The selection of administrators should involve faculties so that people who are academically *persona-non-grata* will not be chosen. But, the process should not give the faculty total control over the selection. The president or chancellor, if he is basically qualified through experience or training to be an academic leader, must be responsible to the governing board. In the case of middle-level administrators, they must be responsible to the president or chancellor.

A second problem is a desire of many faculties to deal with the governing board directly and to either end-run or ignore the responsible administrators involved. Obviously, no one wants absolute insulation between a board of control and members of the faculty. Indeed, some boards have admitted individual faculty representatives, from both their own and other institutions, with salutary effect. However, we believe that for an institution to use its faculty on its own governing board, particularly in a large institution or system, can lead to an impossible administrative impasse. If anything goes wrong, no one is ultimately responsible; there is no way, therefore, to correct or improve awkward situations or outright errors.

A third cause of tension between faculty and administration is administrative arbitrariness and refusal to consider the faculty point of view in areas where administration has clear authority or veto power. There is, of course, no excuse for this, and if the college lets the condition persist, it may lead the faculty to seek a union to negotiate its rights. It is to obviate the dictatorial administrator, who would be guilty of this approach, that faculty and student consultation in administrative appointments has been established. This type of one-man rule is most common in the small president-centered private college and is rapidly going out of style. Certainly no president, dean, or chancellor in a large public system, aware of the complex of pressures upon him, can afford to operate in this manner for very long. Where it happens, however, faculty members have a legitimate protest, and action by the board and not pressure by a union is the corrective we recommend.

WHAT IS THE ACADEMIC SENATE?

The representative group concept deserves separate considera- tion in any discussion of faculty-administration relationships. Whether it is called a faculty council, an advisory board, or an academic senate, a group comprised of elected faculty represen- tatives, and increasingly student representatives, in an organiza- tion which advises the president or chancellor, is capable of solving many problems—and also creating others. The lack of such a group forces faculty members to resort to other less desirable means of having themselves heard, particularly if the administration is dictatorial or unilaterally inclined. In the California State University and Colleges, for example, the absence of academic senates for many years forced the faculties into union- type organizations which became in some cases politically activist and militant. Some of these organizations have been helpful and have aided in the development of the State Colleges; others have been harmful by intervening unnecessarily between legislature, the board of control, and the public.

Administrators and boards must be constantly alert to prevent the gradual erosion of administrative responsibility and trustee authority through the constant pushing of faculty activists. The senates which prefer to operate at a professional level, and through advice and counsel to the responsible executives and boards, can and do serve their institutions well. Their great contribution is found in mobilizing academic influence where and when needed. In the case of major educational issues, some of which administrators become aware of only after the issues have acquired unfortunate proportions, senates can provide sound judgment and helpful advice. They are most effective in such areas as curriculum design and personnel policies. Elected faculty groups can also serve as high courts for adjudication of infractions of professional ethics. They should take the leadership in defining professional ethics as applied to their particular faculty organization. The value of such groups far outweighs their disadvantages. As institutions grow larger and achieve more political connotations, faculty senates and councils are destined to greatly increase in importance. It will be to the advantage of American higher education if all educators cooperate and insure that this elective principle of professional and democratic representation is wisely guided. Faculty members themselves have the largest stake in this development and should realize the hazards to them and their profession inherent in exorbitant demands for administrative authority.

No discussion of faculty-administration relationships would be complete without attention being given to two other principles, both under serious attack at the present time. One of these —the principle of accountability—holds that the person with authority to make decisions must be *accountable* so that he can answer for the quality of the decisions made. The second principle is that an academic institution should function as a *professional* organization, not a political one. Both of these ideas, or

ideals, deserve further amplification; we shall mention briefly
some of the problems inherent in each.

WHAT IS THE PRINCIPLE OF
ACCOUNTABILITY?

Currently, many faculty leaders, particularly those interested
in increasing the amount of delegated authority to elected faculty senates and councils, are arguing that a university or a
college cannot and should not be organized similar to a business
corporation, wherein executives make decisions and are accountable to a board of control. The basis of their criticism is that an
academic organization has its decision-making process so scat-
tered that scores of people are already involved, and it is even
now impossible to pin down responsibility for what goes on.
The fallacy in this argument is that the same situation exists in
large business corporations. There the principle of accountability
is rigidly enforced because boards must hold executives responsible. This managerial axiom prevails even if the size of the
organization renders top decision-making exceedingly difficult in
the face of certain types of organizational complexity. In other
words, the leverage must be there for the executives to bring
about change even though the actualities of the situation militate
against strict interpretation of the principle of accountability.

The arguments for accountability in higher education are very
clear and simple. The general public which provides the funds,
either through gifts, grants, and bequests for private institutions,
or through taxes for public colleges and universities, rightfully
insists on some accounting for its funds. It insists, also, that
someone be held responsible for any misuse of them. A board
of trustees or regents has difficulty grappling with the problems
inherent in the fulfillment of its responsibility—that of setting
the major direction of the institution—if it cannot localize its

control through certain individuals who have decision-making power. The faculty, too, can benefit by having responsibility focused in accountable officials, because when things go wrong, it is not only management that suffers.

A professor who enjoys tenure cannot be held accountable for other than his academic actions. Therefore, no administrator should have tenure, nor should important administrative decisions be made by faculty who do not occupy accountable administrative positions. If higher education permits itself to be lured away from this clear-cut concept, it will soon lose its effectiveness and its support.

HOW DO ACADEMIC POLITICS DIFFER FROM PROFESSIONALISM?

The second principle is that an academic institution should be run as a professional organization; not as a political organism. This also, like the doctrine of accountability, seems simple and obvious. With the growing size of universities and systems, however, this principle could be eroded. The Berkeley upheavals, followed by the period of general student unrest around the country, demonstrated how easily a great institution of higher education (solid, reputable, and venerable) could be completely disrupted by political activism on the part of a minority of students. The obvious success of militancy, whether in connection with the civil rights movement or the reduction of supermarket prices, is encouraging students and other groups to adopt it as a means of achieving their ends.

The questionable stand of some political scientists on these riots and demonstrations is that they constitute normal, if overt, expressions in any democracy. One answer to that argument is that academic institutions are by their very nature based on the principle of selectivity and recognition of the superior. They should operate as professional organizations. Each is a community of scholars working together selflessly for the best interests of the whole. But this pattern is unfortunately changing. At Berkeley and elsewhere, pressure groups managed to divide students, faculty, administrators, and board members. Labor organizers are agitating for faculty unions and collective bargaining so that negotiation for salary and even academic programming may well become subject to public negotiations. At that point, they will be more influenced by the dramatics of the press and the communications media than by the validity of the issues involved. Although unions are active on many campuses and have a strong foothold at others, we are very much concerned for the future of American higher education if it becomes subject to the pressures of unions and political organizations internally as well as externally. Traditional academic freedom will disappear if this occurs. Political militancy and control by pressure groups leave no room for the professor as an individual, as a scholar, as a scientist. In the long run, faculty members, both individually and collectively, have much more to lose than to gain when union negotiations replace the traditional decision-making process.

The answer to this problem is not simple, but it is clear. Educators, both faculty and administrators, must join with students and trustees in seeking better methods for achieving full representation of all valid viewpoints in providing the finest kind of higher education in America.

Justice Learned Hand pointed out that, ". . . you may not carry a sword beneath a scholar's gown, or lead flaming causes from a cloister."[2] If you do, you soon lose the benefits of the unique position which the scholar's gown has traditionally provided. Society has given universities academic freedom because of their willingness selflessly to be objective about matters of concern to society. Once institutions of higher education cease to be objective about these concerns and become participants in the militancies of the political arena, then academic freedom will surely and inevitably disappear.

On a more ephemeral and aesthetic aspect of the problem—on taste and style—if colleges and universities are supposed to lift humanity to its highest levels, then their methods and techniques should be worthy of respect. Any unprofessional conduct or questionable devices used to influence or control public opinion, such as partisan politics and the pitiful beatnik pressure groups, should be beneath the dignity of academic people. If such approaches are not disdained, higher education will sell its birthright, as Justice Hand has said, for a mess of pottage. President Eisenhower illustrated the value of good *taste*; President Kennedy demonstrated the inspirational force of *style*. Higher education has had taste and style, and these have helped it to enjoy the unstinting support of the American people. If it surrenders to bad taste and shoddy style at this juncture, the American people will reject it and withdraw the confidence and the faith which it has enjoyed for more than three centuries.

DOCUMENTATION AND COMMENTARY

1. Alexander Vavoulis, "Delegation of Authority, Fact or Myth in University Government," *The Voice of the Faculties*, Association of California State College Professors, October, 1966, 5.

2. Learned Hand, *The Spirit of Liberty*, New York: Vintage Books, 1959, 105.

12 RETENTION OF THE FACULTY

The question of the retention of faculty members is one of the most important decisions to be made by an institution of higher education. In fact the very quality of the institution depends more upon how this decision is made than upon any other. The integrity and determination with which retention and tenure decisions are made are the measure of the university's vitality. A strong institution makes retention and tenure serious hurdles. A weak institution makes them automatic dividends in return for longevity or survival.

WHAT ARE TENURE AND RETENTION?

Tenure is contractual time. Indefinite tenure refers to a legal agreement wherein the institution contracts with the professor to retain him indefinitely or until he reaches retirement age. In common practice, faculty are hired on a yearly basis until their worth is proven. At that time they are granted tenure and assumed to be permanent employees of the institution.

The determination of retention and tenure is accomplished

under many different patterns, but ordinarily in large high-quality institutions of education, the faculty plays a major role. The department chairman will recommend to a departmental or divisional or college-wide retention and tenure committee in respect to an individual, and the committee will then recommend to the dean or to the president, who has the final word. In some institutions the board retains *pro forma* decision-making power over tenure, but even this is gradually changing and is moving downward to the faculty ranks.

The question of when tenure is granted is a most interesting one and also provides a variety of patterns in practice. The American Association of University Professors has a general rule that tenure shall be granted within seven years or earlier if possible, but that the institution if it desires it shall have seven years in which to decide whether or not it wishes to marry itself permanently to a faculty member. Institutions of lesser quality or those which are subject more directly to political pressures have much shorter probationary periods.

The importance of the tenure decision is even greater when it is realized that it is a completely one-sided contract. The institution commits itself and makes itself legally liable to provide permanent employment for the faculty member. The faculty member, however, need feel no compunction about returning the favor and may at any time pack up and leave. The commitment, therefore, is unilateral, and the institution must be careful to protect itself because of this fact.

Ordinarily, when tenure is granted it is accompanied by a letter of understanding which in the academic world has the effect of a legal and binding contract. During the probationary period it is common to give instructors one-year appointments in writing so that it is clear that they are not on tenure and that their employment carries with it no implication of permanence.

WHY HAVE PROBATIONARY PERIODS?

Some employee organizations are engaged in a constant drive to shorten the probationary period, with the ultimate objective of having tenure in effect granted on recruitment, and secondly to insist that if a probationary employee is not retained, the employer be required to give reasons. If the probationary period means anything in terms of protection for the institution, the employer should not be forced to give reasons. The mere fact that a man is denied a subsequent annual contract during his probationary period does not imply that he is necessarily incompetent; it may merely mean that his aptitudes do not fit within that particular department or that his specialties do not fit the needs of the institution. In any case, no reasons should be required, no reasons should be stated, and the probationary period should be retained as a meaningful period of assessment in which the institution can decide freely whether or not it wishes to tie itself permanently to an individual.

The seriousness of the decision may also be measured in terms of the fiscal commitment. If the average age of an individual being granted tenure is 30, then he might expect 35 years of gainful employment at an average annual salary of say $20,000. It is easy to see that one is here talking about a commitment of two-thirds of a million dollars!

It is easy to be over-lenient in the tenure determination. A man with a family, financial obligations, and an agreeable personality is capable of engendering much sympathetic support whether or not he gives promise of becoming either a great scholar or a great teacher. Furthermore, it is difficult to evaluate teaching ability, and in many cases a man will be given credit for effectiveness which he does not possess because the teaching profession has simply never confronted the issue of evaluating teaching effectively. Also there is occasionally a problem of weaker members of the department wishing to see mediocre individuals given permanence so that there will be no danger of stronger people entering and threatening their own positions and reputations. This problem is a much greater one than is commonly realized and can be cured only by maintaining a role for the administration in the tenure-determination process. On the other hand, a strong department will breed strength, and the administration seldom, if ever, has to enter into the tenure determination of a department whose scholarly and professional reputation is a matter of pride and concern.

IS THERE A SALARY PROBLEM?

Salaries are a matter of serious concern among the faculty today. This was simply not the case a quarter of a century ago. People went into teaching for compensations other than money, and it is only in more recent years that the appeal of salary has become so strong. Even today, there is a visible strain of idealism among faculty members. Salaries do not always represent the vital factor that faculty politicians imply. Nevertheless, money is important, and its importance is signified by the fact that the American people have finally recognized the importance of gifted teachers. Thus salaries have increased proportionately over the last several years to a point where academic people are now reasonably compensated. Their remuneration still cannot compete with that in other professions, but there are compensations which equalize this.

One of the neutralizing factors is that faculty members enjoy a situation in which a mediocre practitioner of his profession in academics can be confident of proportionately higher return than the mediocre practitioner of law or medicine. There is also a time schedule which gives the academic person many professional advantages. His work load, although heavy if he is a competent professor, is nevertheless ordinarily of his own making except for class meetings and office appointments. His summers and holidays provide extra time for consulting, other professional work, or refreshing himself in his subject. Furthermore, if tenured he is more secure in teaching than in any profession outside the federal civil service. Once tenure is granted, whether or not he produces, he has a life-long appointment, and his income is absolutely secure. The fact that not many professors take excessive advantage of this situation is a testimony to the general high quality of individuals in higher education.

A second lure to retain an able faculty is fringe benefits. Fringe benefits can include any number of items, starting with a good retirement system, sick benefits, hospital insurance, and other types of protection. But they also include such items as travel funds to meetings of professional associations, funds so that certain types of jobs can be done (such as manuscript typing), tuition remission programs for family members, and sabbatical leaves. Those who have dealt in educational administration over a long period of time agree generally that fringe benefits are less costly to the institution and generally provide more satisfactions to the faculty member than salary increases involving the same number of dollars. They are, in other words, an inexpensive way to buy high morale. Private institutions have recognized this for many years. Public institutions unfortunately find it much more difficult to have adequate fringe benefit programs because of the possibility of political capital being made from miniscule savings.

ARE WORKING CONDITIONS FAVORABLE?

A third factor which figures in faculty members' decisions to stay or leave at a certain institution is the flexibility of the teaching load. The twelve-hour teaching load which used to be common practice across the nation has been reduced to the point where many institutions are operating with either an eight- or nine-unit average. In our opinion, however, the key to this problem is not so much the establishment of a fixed average for all faculty members, but rather the possibility of flexibly administering teaching loads so that a faculty member who desires a lower class load for a period of time can be given it if he justifies this concession by his research output. Thus, a faculty member who prefers to concentrate on teaching can be given a proportionately larger number of class units. The possibility of a faculty member, however, going to a dean or president and presenting a case for a lower teaching load with the chance of the request's being granted is an item which is extremely important in the minds of faculty.

Another factor which leads to high morale is adequate technical, secretarial, and clerical assistance so that professional faculty are not required to do work which is commonly defined as clerical. A tremendous amount of high-cost professional time is wasted by institutions which try to save a few dollars by forcing faculty members to type their own correspondence and reports, or clean up their own laboratories. Such savings are penny wise and pound foolish. Until the onset of the current financial dilemma, private institutions have been able to meet this problem more easily than public institutions. The latter find it difficult to allocate adequate funds for such items unless the relationship with the state is such that these fiscal decisions can be made at the administrative or board level, rather than with the appropriations committee of the legislature.

Looming large in the minds of faculty members is the attitude of the administration toward the individual professor. If the administration is understanding, approachable, and willing to discuss certain professional problems, the atmosphere of the institution is permissive, and this can often compensate for low salaries and less than average fringe benefits. One of the major factors here is the establishment by the administration of a set of rules and procedures which guarantee fairness in the treatment of professional problems, grievances, appeals, retentions, promotions, and severance. If such decisions and procedures are arbitrary and depend on the whim of the individual administrator, the faculty member is often not favorably impressed, no matter how reputable the institution. Unfortunately, it is in situations such as this that those favoring unionization of the faculty are able to make the most headway in establishing their case. However, if adequate procedures are in existence and if the administration demonstrates that it is willing to follow them, a favorable climate can be maintained without unions.

WHAT IS PROFESSIONAL ETHOS?

Perhaps the most important of all the ties that bind faculty to their college or university is the professional climate of the institution. This is an intangible thing—not only hard to define, but frequently hard to come by. In some cases, a college or university will achieve it easily and quickly. In other cases, it must be planned for carefully. In still other cases, even though carefully planned, it will not be achieved. It consists partly of an item of tremendous importance in the academic world—prestige or status. If the reputation of an institution is one which attracts and holds scholars, which encourages them to develop professionally, which stimulates and encourages gifted teaching, and which attracts and holds able students, then this climate of professionalism is in existence. If the institution is turbulent and disaffected, if it insists on washing its dirty linen in public, if factionalism divides its professional groups, and if rigidities in administration are maintained against the urgings of educational leadership, then obviously it is difficult to establish and maintain a professional climate which will be conducive to improving the quality of the institution. The professional climate, atmosphere, or ethos should be carefully studied. Where it does not exist, an effort should be made to achieve it. For it, more than anything else, including unions, will induce good faculty members to remain on the job.

13 SALARY AND BENEFITS

There has been a change in the attitude of faculties toward the salary problem in recent years. Historically and traditionally the monetary compensation for a professor was seldom considered a major factor in his decision to enter the profession. It was taken for granted that he would live a life of genteel poverty and make up for his low income by a sense of dedication which would give him great moral and spiritual satisfaction. In many instances this turned out to be largely the case. Not many individuals in our total population became college professors, because higher education was not considered to be that popular, remunerative, or important. Many of those who did enter it accepted their responsibilities with an air of resignation as to financial reward. Even today there are many gifted and devoted teachers working in small private institutions, which are unable to pay their faculties prevailing salary scales; however, these teachers are gaining their personal and professional satisfactions through a high sense of dedication to their calling.

WHAT ARE THE CHANGES IN ATTITUDES
TOWARD SALARIES?

There has been, however, a marked change in faculty attitudes toward monetary compensation, due largely to the sudden rise in importance of higher education as a factor in national policy. Since Sputnik in 1957, higher education in this nation has become of increasing concern to everyone. It is growing with fantastic and astronomical rapidity. The federal government's attention to it has given its practitioners a new sense of importance, and everyone seems to agree that it is a most crucial item in American life. This change in national attitudes has, of course, affected the faculties. Many professors, having spent so long in a monetary limbo, now are becoming perhaps overly interested in the financial remuneration of their calling. As discussed in an earlier chapter, in many instances this can lead to the organization of faculty unions, with a resulting increase of interest in collective bargaining, and the encouragement of a militancy on the part of faculty toward salaries and fringe benefits that never before was a part of its professional make-up.

The increase in overt interest and militancy may lose for faculties the sympathy and respect which their air of resignation and dedication gained for them over the years. This is the kind of sympathy and respect, or admiration and affection, that the public so generously accords ministers of the gospel and priests of the church. Any change in public attitude, as a result of changed faculty attitudes will have its effect on legislation in public institutions and on donors in private institutions.

WHAT ARE THE PROBLEMS OF
SALARY IMPROVEMENT?

Although salaries continue to be a matter of concern they are much better today than they ever were before. In fact, salaries of college professors have gone up faster than have incomes of other professions over the last decade. Today a practitioner in the field of higher education, if he is capable, can expect a reasonable income. Salaries are still not so high as the top professional incomes of the leading practitioners of medicine or law, but on the other hand the averages are far higher than the incomes of mediocre practitioners of those two professions. Progress has been made, but this matter of remuneration is beset with many problems.

One of these problems is that with the advent of unions many people think that faculty members have lost the sense of dedication and selflessness which was so important in the creation of an outstanding teacher. This is not necessarily true, but higher salaries, fringe benefits, and special prerequisites are bringing into the profession many individuals who three or four decades ago would never have thought of going into college teaching.

Another problem is that the increase in faculty salaries has added enormously to the fiscal burdens of both private and public institutions. The public higher education budgets in most state systems, and indeed the budgets of most private colleges, are primarily taken up in faculty compensation of one sort or another. In very recent years, it has, therefore, become necessary for many institutions to reduce the rate of salary increase, and in some instances to provide no increase.

IS STRUCTURING OF SALARY SCALES DESIRABLE?

There are several ways in which to create salary scales, and all of them have been used at one time or another by various colleges and universities.

One method is to develop a list of comparison institutions with which one's own salaries are contrasted. This is the way in

which the California State University and Colleges' salary budgets are fixed by the Coordinating Council and the legislature.
There are several problems involved in this approach, the chief
of which is the difficulty of finding institutions which are truly
comparable. Obviously any college or university wants to feel
that it is to be compared with the best, and this is not always
acceptable to the fiscal authorities. Where it is, of course, it constitutes a very sound and easy method of establishing salary levels.

The comparison principle has also been applied in recent
striving to have higher educational salaries compare favorably
with those in other professions. There are many arguments favoring this approach, the most logical of which is that the holder
of a Ph.D. goes through an educational process which is just
about as long and difficult as that faced by any of the other
major professions, and his period of apprenticeship is also lengthy
and arduous. The chief argument against it is that unlike other
professions, in which most of the practitioners are self-employed,
the college professor has absolute security, long vacations in
which to keep himself professionally alive, and, once he has
achieved a full professorship and tenure in a good institution,
no further need to compete against his colleagues. These latter
arguments are very appealing to legislators and board members.
They are the chief reason for the refusal, up to the present, to
have faculty salaries match those of top medical and legal
incomes.

A second method of calculating faculty salaries is that of trend
lines, and this is often used in conjunction with the comparison
approach. The American Association of University Professors has
carefully studied faculty salaries for several years and has calculated reasonably dependable percentages of annual increase
which colleges and universities can use to good effect in asking
for salary increases on a blanket basis. Cost of living increases

also can be projected by using trend lines from federal statistical data.

WHAT ABOUT DISTRIBUTION
OF SALARY FUNDS?

Once acquired, salary money can be distributed in several different ways. The simplest, of course, is for the president or dean arbitrarily to determine who should get what. This was a popular technique in small private colleges for many years. Because faculty salaries were not a major academic issue, administrators were successful with it. Today, however, conditions are changing to the extent that it is unlikely that this approach can or should be continued much longer.

The distribution of salary funds is a major topic in the question of establishing faculty unions on campus. Those professors who favor unionization believe that the unions could effectively use collective bargaining as a means of negotiating salaries with the administration. Although such techniques may result in short-term increases in salaries and fringe benefits, there is no question but that these material gains will come about only at the expense of traditional professional freedoms. Therefore, we recommend that faculties considering the question of collective bargaining as a means of negotiating salaries and fringe benefits do so with caution. As we suggested in earlier sections of this volume, the short term monetary gains will cost more professionally than the faculty may initially realize. When this occurs faculty members may well be reduced to the status of mere employees of the institution instead of being a major controlling factor in institutional governance as they are now.

A better method than collective bargaining is to maintain salary scales with some flexibility in terms of the faculty's and the administration's judgment as to quality or merit of individ-

uals. If it is known, for instance, that an assistant professor
receives a certain range of compensation, then the more competent individuals or the more senior ones can have higher compensation within that range without making others on the
faculty feel that inequities are inevitable.

An interesting paradox exists in the faculty mind. On one
hand, the professor insists on being treated as a detached professional; on the other, he is resentful if certain colleagues who
are genuinely gifted and productive are compensated more generously than is he. We recognize that this paradox creates
stresses, strains, and tensions in faculty-administration relationships and even between associates in the same division, department, or discipline. However, it is doubtful that in the long
run unions and collective bargaining will be a satisfactory means
of solving this dilemma.

Another problem in applying salary money is whether the
salaries should be published or confidential. It is our feeling that
his salary should be a man's personal concern, and only the levels
or ranges, not the individual salaries, should be published, even
in public institutions. Unfortunately, line item budgets, especially in public institutions, do not always permit this sort of
consideration for the individual. In many cases salaries become
a matter of public record and, as might be expected, public
comment.

WHAT ARE THE ADVANTAGES OF
A GOOD SALARY SCALE?

The advantages of a generous and sound salary scale are
many and are evident. In the first place, it enables the institution to recruit faculty of high quality. Secondly, it enables their
long-term retention. Thirdly, it permits a more stable faculty
body and encourages more loyalty to the institution. Finally,

and of equal importance, is the fact that if a professor is generously compensated, the administration and the board have a
right to expect more of him than of a professor who is constantly irritated because of what he feels is inadequate compensation. This also has a fundamental effect on the general academic
quality of the institution.

ARE FRINGE BENEFITS IMPORTANT?

The area of fringe benefits constitutes a most interesting and
seldom understood part of the obligation of an institution to its
faculty. Many private institutions have learned that well selected
and generous fringe benefits provide a relatively inexpensive
way of additionally compensating faculty and maintaining good
morale. In some cases a sound fringe benefit system will help to
make up for a basically inadequate salary scale. In the past, the
small private institution has had a definite advantage over the
large public one with restricted funds, because relatively generous arrangements could be made for such things as paid up
insurance, and housing, which often introduced categories which
legislatures and state fiscal authorities were unwilling to con-
template. However, current financial conditions have restricted
even the private college's ability to provide these benefits.

There are many types of fringe benefits: retirement, housing,
health insurance, educational privileges for faculty families, such
as tuition exchanges, loans, and emergency funds. Also provided
are such financial aids as moving expenses, recreational advantages, leaves (both paid and non-paid), faculty travel, parking
advantages on urban campuses, secretarial help, faculty clubs,
and special facilities for faculty gatherings and meals.

Regarding fringe benefits, Ingraham and King have observed
that, "The most important compensation of a faculty member
is the opportunity to do pleasant and useful work under condi-

tions that make it effective, and to live in a community of scholars without incurring undue economic hardship for either himself or his family. Therefore we insure first the conditions that make a scholar's work effective. These include library facilities, equipment, students, and a schedule of work that does not preclude performance of high quality. These also involve academic freedom, tenure, and administrative understanding. But in addition to these, a degree of economic security is vital. Salary, retirement provisions, and various types of insurance are of major importance in this regard. However, other prerequisites may be of great value and under certain circumstances prove of comparable importance with any benefits other than working conditions and salary. . . . Some staff benefits are largely means of compensating the faculty in ways that give them more than if the equivalent in cost were paid in salary. These may result in savings to the faculty because of the lesser cost of doing things on a group basis than on an individual one or because of savings through use of the institution's favorable purchasing power. Examples are low rentals, low interest mortgage loans, family education privileges, campus hospital and medical services, and purchases through the university. Others are facilities of minor pecuniary importance but affording conveniences or pleasant privileges, e.g. faculty club, athletic privileges, preferential treatment in regard to attendance at lectures, concerts, athletic events, and perhaps parking. Other items represented part conditions of work and part staff benefits, such as travel expenses and research leaves. Personal loans to meet family exigencies are hard to classify."[1]

DOCUMENTATION AND COMMENTARY

1. Mark H. Ingraham and Francis P. King, *The Outer Fringe—Faculty Benefits Other Than Annuities and Insurance*, Madison, Wisconsin: The University of Wisconsin Press, 1965, 3, 5. (Study for the Commission on Faculty and Staff Benefits for the Association of American Colleges)

14 PROMOTION PROCEDURES

It has been said that soldiers fight for medals, not for money, and the pageantry of the academic procession with the colorful caps, gowns, hoods, and protocol, although openly derided by many faculty members, is secretly a source of satisfaction for most of them. In addition, the traditional ranks of faculty—instructor, assistant professor, associate professor, and full professor —constitute a pattern of professional advancement which for many decades has compensated the professor, in part at least, for what he has lacked in monetary income.

Part of this concern over rank was inherited from the German universities where the Herr Professor was a rank not easily arrived at and, once achieved, carried with it tremendous social, civic, and political prominence. American colleges and universities have largely robbed the rank of full professor of much of its prestige by making it too often a prize for longevity rather than achievement, but it still has an aura of sanctity about it in the academic profession.

WHAT IS THE PROCESS OF PROMOTION?

In most institutions of higher education the faculty plays a prominent role in the promotion process. The department ordinarily makes recommendations to the chairman as to which of its members should be recognized by promotion, and if the department is large enough, this may well be done by a special committee assigned the job of evaluating individuals for promotion. The department chairman then carries his recommendations to the dean, who in some cases has the final word, or to the president. In some universities there is a college or university-wide promotion committee which receives recommendations from departments and then evaluates them in a lengthy, time-consuming, and difficult process before they are recommended to the responsible administrative officer. Most promotion committees, whether departmental or college-wide, operate very conscientiously and at a high professional level. The task of recommending colleagues for promotion is taken very seriously by most academic people, and a post on the promotion committee is a mark of high confidence by one's academic colleagues.

In some colleges today there are student members on committees assigned the responsibility of determining which members of the faculty are to be promoted. Our opinion is that although student evaluation of some aspects of a professor's work should be sought and given serious consideration, students should make recommendations only on such matters and should not be voting members of the promotion committee. It seems to us that students do not have the experience, nor do they know enough about a faculty member's total contribution and value to the institution and his profession, to be responsible for such an important decision.

The president plays a major role in promotion, in some small institutions, largely because the process is closely related to the budget, and the tighter the budget, the more concerned the president is with processes that affect it. But, by and large, the system of having a single administrator, or even a group of administrators, judge which members of the faculty are fit for professional recognition has gone out of style. We believe that the fairest, most logical, and most equitable process is to have the final decisions on promotion made by one's peers, with input from other members of the college community to the extent they are able to provide accurate and helpful information.

WHAT ARE PROMOTION CRITERIA?

The criteria for promotion vary from institution to institution but are singularly consistant throughout higher education. There are usually three areas of concern—teaching, research, and service—which are examined in connection with an individual's claim to advancement. All three of these, along with advisement and committee assignments, were discussed in Section One of the book. By all odds the most difficult area to evaluate fairly and thoroughly is teaching ability. Even major research institutions consider teaching ability to be important, and generally include it in their list of qualifications for retention, tenure, and promotion. Even if the professor concentrated chiefly on research, his ability to transmit knowledge to students in an effective manner counts in terms of his professional recognition. However, as we said in an earlier chapter, the problem with teaching is that it is at best extremely difficult to measure and to evaluate effectively.[1] Thus the tendency is for administrators and other responsible for faculty evaluation to assign greater weight to other areas, such as research and publishing, when attempting to determine an individual professor's work.

The reason we have so much trouble evaluating teaching is that we have never agreed on what a proper outcome of teaching should be. If the goal of the institution is to place as many students as possible in graduate school and to have them succeed there, then superior teaching in that institution consists of turning out successful graduate students. On the other hand, if the goal of the institution is to turn out good citizens who will enter into business, government service, and other occupations immediately following graduation, then another set of standards must be developed. To carry the problem one step further, how is good citizenship measured—by economic success or by participation in civic activity or by a sound and wholesome family life and church membership? In any case, even if we could agree on the proper outcomes of good teaching, the professor would be long since dead before we would have enough evidence to apply to his request for promotion if teaching ability is to be basically considered as the qualification for advancement.

A second prerequisite for promotion in most institutions of higher education is some demonstrated proficiency in scholarship in connection with the individual's academic discipline. A historian or a literary expert is expected to publish; an artist is expected to produce creative works which are recognized for their quality; an individual in teacher education might make an adequate reputation for himself by extensive consultation with school districts or by demonstrating leadership qualities in the educational fraternity. In any case, professional achievement is a part of the requirement for promotion. Of all of the qualifications, it is the most easily measured, and consequently the most frequently abused. It is relatively simple to detect whether or not a historian is respected by his colleagues and enjoys a reputation which goes beyond the immediate institution or locality. It is even easier to tell whether or not a scientist has made his mark in terms of research results. Sometimes, of course, sheer volume of product is mistaken for quality of output, but generally faculty committees and administrators find the evaluation of scholarly achievement a relatively easy task.

A third requirement for promotion in most colleges and universities is service to the institution and/or the community. This merely means that the professor must show he is a good citizen, does not object too loudly or vocally to committee assignments, and demonstrates he is interested one way or another in the welfare of the institution and its place in its city or region. True, this type of record is not always the kind favored by administrators. In some cases faculty members who have been thorns in the flesh of administration are gleefully recognized by their colleagues as having performed signal services by leading movements for salary increases, acting as spokesman in militant drives for faculty rights, and in other ways disturbing the repose of well-intentioned college presidents. But, by and large, service to the college or community is also rather easily measured and presents no great difficulty as a basis for promotion.

WHO MAKES RECOMMENDATIONS
FOR PROMOTION?

Once the criteria for promotion are decided on, the next job is to determine who is to be consulted in applying them to the individual who is a candidate for advancement. Faculties have a simple, all-inclusive answer to this. It consists of what is known as peer judgment or evaluation by professional colleagues. If faculty members occasionally visited each other's classes they would have an objective basis upon which to judge a colleague's fitness for promotion. The time is long overdue when department heads and deans should be making such visits for evaluative purposes. Composite or collective evaluations, although frowned upon as a sole determinant in most faculty circles, ordinarily enter the picture somewhere along the line.

One area in which students can make a positive contribution to faculty evaluation is in the evaluation of a professor's teaching ability. Large numbers of colleges and universities across the country have already developed a variety of programs for this purpose, and many are in the process of doing so. Also, several independent agencies supported by foundation grants are developing student evaluation procedures and evaluation forms. In some cases the evaluation is done on a strictly voluntary basis, and professors who do not wish to risk this type of judgment are free to refuse. In other institutions, students have taken it upon themselves to do some independent judging, and certain colleges and universities now have lists published by the students at their own expense with exceedingly frank evaluations of members of the faculty. As might be expected, in some cases these are extremely accurate and valuable and in other cases not worth the trouble to read.

While we agree that students attending college now have something to contribute to the evaluation process, particularly in connection with teaching ability, often overlooked is that their qualifications for judgment may actually be better after they have left the institution and are in a position to look back upon their entire educational career and view it in perspective. What they regard as outstanding teaching when they were freshmen or sophomores might appear to them as graduates to have been largely a waste of time. Although the popular, friendly professor might have been given good marks by undergraduates, these same students, when they got to graduate school or into business, may have changed their views and rated the tough professor much more highly. Thus, although student evaluations are useful, we suggest that alumni, especially recent alumni, may also be a valuable source of evaluative information.

Administrators, also, despite the dim view which many faculty take, have something to contribute to this process. An administrator is probably even better qualified to judge in the area of institutional and community service than are faculty colleagues. Most administrators, having come up through the ranks themselves, are reasonably adept in evaluating a person in terms of teaching ability and scholarship, if only from the complaints, praise, and comments that form a constant part of the academic grapevine.

In sum, however, the judgments of an academic community about its members are not very scientific, even though they purport to be. They consist of a rather jumbled mass of reactions based on hearsay, the individual's personality, student reports, complaints, colleague criticism or praise, and scholarly production.

WHAT ARE THE PROBLEMS OF PROMOTION?

There are several problems in connection with the promotional process which need brief review. One of these problems is the tendency on the part of many colleges and universities with funds in short supply to use academic rank as a substitute for money. This is an extremely unfortunate practice and leads to the downgrading of the academic ranks; and sooner or later it has its effect on the quality of the faculty as a whole. Yet this is a very easy trap for administrators to fall into. Coupling an inadequate financial raise with an increase in rank makes it palatable and keeps the faculty member quiet, at least temporarily. And because this can be and has been done, legislators and financial officers are often convinced that it can be continued without detriment to the institution. Such is not the case.

Another problem is that certain institutions have percentage limitations of ranks, largely because of fiscal restrictions. In the California State University and Colleges, for instance, the full professorial and associate professorial groups cannot constitute more than 60 per cent of the faculty total, and although this might seem to provide plenty of elbowroom when an institution achieves maturity (particularly after several years of using promotion as a substitute for salary), the possibility for advancement for new members of the faculty appears slim, and this constitutes a most discouraging factor in faculty recruitment. This is not to say that the full professorship should be entirely open-ended, but there should always be opportunity for fully qualified people to move up the ladder. The problem in many American faculties is that people who should never be advanced are often promoted, thus leaving little room for those who should receive the accolade.

Certain faculty organizations and groups have come to the conclusion that promotion represents an undemocratic process and the chief goal of reorganization should be to eliminate promotion completely. Such a plan suggests a single salary scale—one salary for everyone—a single rank, that of full professor, for everyone, and tenure upon recruitment, which would of course eliminate all necessity for invidious choices. Unfortunately not only does this eliminate all possibility of unfairness, it also eliminates all possibility of developing an outstandingly good academic institution, and suggestions of this nature should be rejected out of hand.

Finally, there is the problem of adding a fifth rank to the four, that of distinguished professor. This can be done and is done in many colleges and universities; it is usually restricted to individuals who have achieved great renown in their field. Again, many faculty people frown upon this rank because it represents distinction and incrimination of a sort. But where it is effective and politically possible, it represents an effective way to award merit.

In conclusion, the traditional faculty ranks and the promotional process together provide a means of recognizing the achievement of certain individuals. The tendency in some American institutions of higher education to make the full professorship a reward for survival should be discouraged as thoroughly and decisively as the Germanic tendency to make the full professorship a tiny, closed corporation open only to a handful of the elite. There must be an appropriate middle ground whereby competent people can be rewarded by promotion arrived at by decisions conscientiously made, even if based largely on subjective evaluation. It should be recognized that some individuals will never rise above certain ranks, simply because their professional achievements do not compare favorably with those of their colleagues. Promotion ought to mean something important to every faculty member, and the appointment to the rank of full professor in a distinguished institution of higher learning should be the capstone of a professional career.

DOCUMENTATION AND COMMENTARY

1. For a comprehensive and thorough treatment of the entire topic of faculty evaluation, the reader is referred to Richard I. Miller, *Evaluating Faculty Performance*, San Francisco: Jossey-Bass, Inc., Publishers, 1972.

15 SABBATICALS AND PERSONAL DEVELOPMENT

Faculty members are no different than any other group of people in their desire to live the good life. Two of the ways in which they fulfill this desire are through obtaining time off and achieving new status. Through sabbaticals and leaves of absence, both aims are met, since the result is usually increased personal and professional development.

WHAT ARE SABBATICALS?

Sabbaticals originated for faculty members as time off—usually a full year at half pay—for purposes of rest, relaxation, change of pace, and scholarly refurbishment. While the first three purposes were inherent in the leave, its primary purpose was for study. It was felt originally that instructors and professors needed and deserved opportunity to get away from their students, and even from their campus, in order to renew and expand their knowledge of their subjects.

Now, however, the first three purposes prevail, with a different fourth purpose—extra compensation—added. Sometimes both fourth purposes are obtained. Certainly if a faculty member takes on a special research project related to his discipline, he gains new knowledge as well as additional remuneration.

The Commission on Faculty and Staff Benefits of the Association of American Colleges has made and published a helpful study of this important matter of leaves of absence. While the study leans heavily in the direction of suggesting maximum benefits without much reference to the cost to the institution, nevertheless it constitutes a significant contribution to thought and practice on this issue. The first paragraph from the study helps set the stage for further consideration: "The college or university teacher should be a scholar who is constantly increasing his knowledge and keeping abreast of the development of his field. Frequently he is an active investigator, and in many institutions research is a significant portion of his obligations. He should remain a man of vigor, with a fresh mind and broad intellectual interests. Heavy teaching duties performed year after year may make this impossible. Leaves of absence and special research assignments at reasonable intervals of time are among the means of assuring that institutions of higher learning have the kind of faculty that they need. A well-developed program of leaves is of major importance in enhancing the professional development of faculty members. Moreover, the work done while the scholar is on leave, for example, through the results of his investigation or his public service, often is of immediate value to society. The health of the faculty members is a constant concern of the college, and leaves are one of the means of protecting it."[1]

There is a fine line between a sabbatical as a right and a sabbatical as a privilege. On the side of the former, tradition and precedence would indicate that because of the intellectual and professional nature of teaching, its practitioners have a right to the physical relaxation and mental renewal implied in the sabbatical concept. On the side of the latter, with the financial situation currently critical, there are those trustees and administrators who consider that faculty members are granted a privilege when they are included in a sabbatical program.

WHO AWARDS LEAVES?

The policy governing sabbaticals and other leaves should be a regular part of the policies of the institution. Originally, it should be formulated by the board of trustees on the recommendation of the president and with the advice of the faculty.

The implementation of the policy, just as the administration of any other facet of the institution's program, should be a responsibility of management, notably the president. Since this is a highly sensitive area, great care should be taken in the initial formulation of the policy, in equitably modifying it to keep it viable both academically and financially, and in fairly administering it under existing guidelines.

While full-year sabbaticals are expensive and must be covered by board and faculty policy, short-term leaves of absence are not costly and should be within the granting power of the president, possibly with the advice of the faculty. Likewise, other brief absences from the campus, especially if requested for professional advancement, should be the concern of the deans and department chairmen.

WHEN ARE THEY GIVEN?

Sabbaticals or long leaves are, or should be, given sparingly and periodically, such as every seven years, as outlined in the institution's policy statements. When withheld or awarded arbitrarily, great confusion and conflict arises.

As the AAC study observes, "In the majority of colleges and

in many universities by far the chief purpose of leaves is to insure that the individual becomes and remains as good a teacher as his capacities permit. The opportunity to keep abreast of rapidly developing fields frequently is needed. Although a leave should have a purpose, it need not always be tightly structured."[2]

In general, long leaves of absence should be granted when earned through length of service. Short leaves of absence should be granted when needed for personal reasons, when deserved because of devoted service, such as the carrying of extra responsibilities, or when they would react to the benefit of students, the faculty, and the institution, such as representation at a learned symposium.

Actually, leaves undertaken for professional advancement—and most should be granted for that purpose, though serving both the personal needs of the individuals and the interests of the institution—are chiefly an investment of society designed to strengthen higher education as well as increase the capabilities of the person and enhance the reputation of the college or university.

Obviously, there are few if any public or private institutions that can ignore the costs in terms of replacements, expense, and continuing remuneration that are brought about by both regular sabbaticals and unscheduled leaves. Thus, the determination of who gets what leave of absence must reside with the administration and be governed by existing and understood institutional directives.

Similarly, leaves should not be considered as deferred compensation to be furnished faculty regardless of other opportunities for professional development, or given to him in cash, or paid to his estate on his death. Every college or university has an obligation to provide opportunities that will expand the professional horizons of its teachers and scholars; institutions have no obligation to increase a faculty member's bank account as a substitute for an increase in his experience and his knowledge.

WHAT OTHER FORMS OF TIME OFF EXIST?

In addition to sabbaticals or regular leaves of absence, there are many other forms of time off. These include standard vacation periods, usually consisting of three months in the summer and three weeks during the academic year. In this matter of long and frequent vacations, it is understood that faculty members can do as they wish with their time, but some expectation of scholarly or cultural activity is legitimate on the part of the employing institution.

Along with regular vacation, it is understood that leaves for illness or emergency purposes occasionally occur. Unless they are of considerable duration, the institution is expected to carry the employee, be he faculty, non-faculty, or administration for the period involved. Among the short-term leaves where salary is negotiable are those where the faculty member initiates the project requiring released time and where he is paid by the sponsoring agency, usually the government, industry, or a foundation.

Faculty members serving in the armed forces are given leave without pay, but frequently their time in service is considered as special purpose, and credit is given toward promotion, tenure, and sabbatical accruals.

WHAT IS THE RESPONSIBILITY
OF FACULTY MEMBERS?

Teachers and researchers have a professional responsibility in this matter of taking time off for growth purposes. All intellectuals need to stay abreast of new knowledge in their field. Additionally they need frequent exposure to other creative minds and cultural experiences. Finally, from the standpoint of personal health and general fitness, they need and deserve an occasional change of pace, relaxation, and recreation.

While faculty members have not been well paid in the past, salaries and benefits are rising to the point where professors, and even instructors, can and should invest in themselves, in terms of arranging for suitable activities that will provide some or all of the three necessary experiences mentioned above.

We should evaluate leaves of absence as necessary from the regular routine of teaching, research, and campus responsibilities. We should urge administrators to assist faculty members in arranging for such time off and in suggesting ways in which some subsidy can be obtained if needed. We should urge faculty to break away for purposes of personal and professional refreshment and intellectual refurbishing. We should urge the foundations, the corporations, and the government to use faculty members on leave for the mutual benefit of all concerned. All of this presumes that the basic responsibilities of the individual will be covered on campus, so that undue burdens will not be placed on the institution, colleagues, or students.

Because education is a social activity in the academic sense, its practitioners have a responsibility to society generally. One aspect of that professional responsibility is to share with others the wisdom accumulated. Mursell says, "The very persistence and vitality of scholarly and professional organizations, whose members may come from great distances for discussion and mutual stimulation, are good evidence that learning is not by nature a purely solitary preoccupation and that the learner in the very act and process of learning behaves always as a social being."[3]

ARE THERE SABBATICALS
FOR ADMINISTRATORS?

It is legitimately argued that faculty members need and de-

serve long leaves—sabbaticals—at least once each decade in order
to review their discipline, catch up on new developments in their
subject, and generally obtain physical, intellectual, and emotional
change of pace. The fact that most of them have three months'
vacation each summer does not negate the desirability from the
point of view of both the individual and the institution, of their
having sabbaticals.

Many institutions are pondering the feasibility of providing
sabbaticals, or at least long leaves of absence, for administrative
officers. The rationale for this is that these presidents, deans, and
directors need exposure to new methods and techniques in their
areas and have much less free time in which to acquire them than
do faculty members.

One of the reasons why enlightened trustees and thoughtful
faculties are proposing sabbaticals for administrators is that most
of these educational executives came up through the various ranks
of the teaching profession and sometimes return to the classroom
and laboratory. When such administrators are granted a sabbatical or leave, they frequently travel, study, or conduct research in
their previous academic or scientific discipline.

WHAT IS THE NEWEST TREND?

It appears that the best investment an institution can make in
this matter of granting leaves is to give them more frequently
to the young than the old. But as the Commission wisely observes, "Both the dire results of fossilization and the outraged
sense of fair-play preclude a great difference between the two."[4]

Thus, to keep peace on campus, most presidents and deans are
currently finding it expedient to balance out this aspect of selection and to implement precisely institutional policy in this area.

Such leaves do not automatically guarantee increased effectiveness, and many scholars are able to continue their professional

growth without leaves. However, nearly every higher institution now has a supported plan of sabbaticals and/or leaves as a major component of its educational or personnel policy. Whatever policy is formulated should recognize that leaves with pay should be arranged so as to equalize opportunities for professional development among the various fields of scholarship and even among different individuals in the same field.

One of the newest and most promising developments in this area is the reverse of administrators' taking leave for scholarly purposes. It is the fact that many teachers are using their sabbaticals for the study or actual practice of administration. Again, this kind of cross-over experience is highly beneficial to all concerned. This provides opportunity for the faculty member to learn some of the problems and potentialities of academic management—thus gaining new insights along with a change of pace—even if he has no intention of leaving the green pastures of professorial status for the limbo of administration!

WHAT ARE SOME MISCELLANEOUS PRINCIPLES ON LEAVES?

Leaves should exceed one year plus contiguous summers only in unusual circumstances. Regardless of the length of the leave, the work of the faculty must be continued.

Persons on leave even for short periods should be encouraged, but not forced, to write for publication. The corollary of this is that faculty members have insufficient time while on regular assignment to do much writing. While we oppose the principle of publish or perish, we suggest more scholarly publishing if and when time permits.

Large departments should plan for a variable number of their members being always on leave. This need not be considered detrimental to the department. Not only may the absent members be gaining new insights, but their replacements may bring forth fresh ideas to the institution.

In most cases, leaves are granted with the understanding that the recipient will return to his institution. However, the regular policy, or other special arrangements, should be fully understood and accepted by the individual and the institution well in advance of the sabbatical or leave.

Benefits such as retirement and insurance premiums, as regular compensation, must be continued while staff members are on leave with pay. An institution's retirement plan should be so organized as to accept voluntary annuity contributions from employees on leaves of absence without pay.

Among the obligations assumed by a faculty member going on leave are the following:

1. To make the request for leave at a reasonable time in advance and through established procedures, except under unusual circumstances.

2. To not accept an appointment elsewhere at a time later than would be considered ethical if he were not on leave.

3. To return from leave of absence when the circumstances of granting the leave indicate that this is the only equitable action—frequently the case when leaves on pay are granted to pursue graduate study. He should, of course, honor any agreement to return which he has made.[5]

DOCUMENTATION AND COMMENTARY

1. "A Statement on Leaves of Absence," *Bulletin of the American Association of University Professors*, September, 1967, 53:5, 270.

2. *Ibid.*, 271.

3. James L. Mursell, *Successful Teaching*, New York: McGraw-Hill Company, 1946, 159.

4. "A Statement on Leaves of Absence," *op. cit.*, 271.

5. *Ibid.*, 274.

16 PROFESSIONAL ETHICS

The question of professional ethics in higher education has always been a matter of concern to conscientious faculty members, and numerous statements have been made and positions taken on it. Occasionally, when incidents occurred which threatened to intrude upon the integrity of the profession, the views of professors regarding appropriate ethics for their operations have been periodically clarified. However, it has never been a matter of critical import for the profession as a whole, primarily because the American people have properly and accurately regarded college professors as a highly respectable group who were able to keep their own house in order. With the exception of occasional unfortunate incidents when politics have threatened to intrude, and in response to which the profession has risen as one to defend itself, higher education has not been seriously concerned with a generally agreed-upon list of principles—although such lists have been produced.

WHAT IS THE CHANGING SIGNIFICANCE OF PROFESSIONAL ETHICS?

Today, the picture is considerably changed. With the rapid growth of higher education, the astronomical expansion of its budgets, and the student and faculty unrest which have plagued many campuses, it has become a matter of serious and immediate concern to citizens and taxpayers. Since Sputnik, higher education has also achieved the status of a factor in national policy. These two developments have encouraged the press and communications media to make it a front-page item, whereas in earlier decades it was never a matter of prime interest for the general public. What higher education does today, and how it does it, is therefore of great importance. Considering the pressures upon higher education, both fiscal and political, the decision is now squarely before it as to whether or not it wishes to continue at a professional level or be forced downward by these pressures to the level of a skilled trade.

There is only one answer to this which can possibly be satisfactory to the profession. It *must* continue at a professional level. It must operate as a *bona fide* profession, with all of the implications for service to humanity which this implies.

WHAT IS A PROFESSION?

What do we mean when we talk about a profession as opposed to a trade or occupation? For one thing we imply that the amount of knowledge and skill is greater and the training period probably longer. In addition, we associate some dignity or status with professional people which is not accorded to most other types of workers. We assume that they will constitute a minority of the population, and we never consider their sheer weight of numbers when we talk about the influence of the professional groups. We also assume, although this will come under some question among college professors, that the professional man or woman is paid somewhat better than his less skilled colleagues, and this is generally true even in the lowest paid professions, such as teaching.

There is one other assumption, although this is not so clear in people's minds as these other more obvious characteristics. It is that professions involve service to mankind and a sense of responsibility and obligation which supersedes, or should supersede, the material gain which practice of the craft involves. Medical doctors have the Hippocratic oath; ministers have the long tradition of service to God and man, which has characterized them for centuries; teachers have their devotion to the service of youth. Webster involves in his first three definitions of the word *profession,* some implication of "devotion" to a cause or service. When he comes to the definition of the term we are concerned with, he says, "the occupation, if not purely commercial, mechanical, agricultural, or the like, to which one devotes oneself; a calling in which one professes to have acquired some special knowledge used by way either of instructing, guiding, or advising others or of serving them in some art. . . ."[1] Funk and Wagnall say the verb *profess,* from which the noun derives, consists in declaring one's devotion to—in other words, there is implied here a relationship with people and a concept of service which is clear and unmistakable. A person is disgraced in his profession through failing to live up to its ideals of service. He is not similarly disgraced in a trade or craft or occupation.

IS EDUCATION A PROFESSION?

Teachers have never been considered very seriously by other professions. Our folklore is full of such witticisms as, "Those who can, do; those who can't, teach; and those who can't teach, teach others to teach." This derogatory attitude is natural, considering that ours is a young nation and young cultures have little time for the regularization or transmission of their culture. They are too much preoccupied with food, shelter, and clothing and with making a living to bother about affairs of the intellect or of learning in general. During colonial days when the lawyers were reading in colleague's offices, families placed their children under the tutelage of ne'er-do-wells who found that the reading was too much for them or under poorly trained traveling schoolmasters who had failed at other occupations and resorted to teaching as a last attempt to keep from starving. Nor were parents worried too much about what the children were taught as long as they were not frankly illiterate. In the simple business of the frontier it was useful to know how to read, write, and figure, but anything beyond that was left to the wealthy sophisticates of the eastern cities who resorted to European schools and colleges if they expected their children to acquire any further polish or cultivation of the mind.

It was, therefore, a difficult job for teachers to raise their craft to professional status, even when it became clear that to make a democracy work, we were going to have to educate tremendous numbers of our young people. The typical rural American school was a one-room affair, with all grades represented, and teaching at such a school required greater knowledge of human relations and physical control techniques than any high level of intellectual or professional achievement.

But professionalism came. It came among the teachers of the elementary and secondary grades, and it has come among the professors in colleges and universities. In 1940, the American Association of University Professors produced a policy document on academic freedom and tenure which included the following statements: "The teacher is entitled to freedom in the classroom in discussing a subject but he should be careful not to introduce into his teaching controversial matter which has no relation to his subject. Limitations of academic freedom because of religious or other aims of the institution should be clearly stated in writing at the time of the appointment."

And further, "The college or university teacher is a citizen, a member of a learned profession and an officer of an educational institution; when he speaks or writes as a citizen, he should be free from institutional censorship or discipline but his special position in the community imposes special obligations. As a man of learning and an educational officer, he should remember that the public may judge his profession and his institution by his utterances. Hence, he should at all times be accurate and should exercise appropriate restraint, should show respect for the opinions of others, and should make every effort to indicate that he is not an institutional spokesman."[2]

WHAT IS THE CURRENT IMPORTANCE OF PROFESSIONALISM?

The reason professional ethics are so fundamentally and critically significant to the academic profession today is that unless professors clearly demonstrate to the public that they are operating in a fully responsible manner, with the concept of service uppermost in their minds, the public and the politicians will be certain to move in with controls that will eventually erode and destroy academic freedom and reduce the teachers' profession to the status of a skilled trade.

We are already aware of the dangers that confront higher education in this regard. If individuals on a campus, students or faculty, attempt to test the tolerance of the community beyond its acceptance point by publications or utterances that are offensive to public morals and taste, legislation is immediately threatened. If violence breaks out on a campus, lawmakers conclude that the only proper solution is external control through law. Obviously, not all of these problems can be solved or prevented by a true professional attitude, but unless the public has full confidence that the academic person is willing and able to cope with them so that external controls do not appear to be necessary, external controls will most certainly be applied.

Another reason for the critical character of this problem at the present time exists in recent developments in academic government. With the creation of the multiversity, with the development of large institutions in which the human being becomes a very small cog, with the necessity for persons of greater managerial than educational experience in positions of top academic authority, the tendency certainly exists for higher education to drift into ways that are absolutely opposed to the continuation of professionalism. Faculty unions and collective bargaining are only one of these threats, but as stated earlier, we are of the opinion that should faculty unions become a general way of life in colleges and universities in this country, college teaching will no longer be a profession. It will degenerate to the status of a skilled trade, and its order and conduct will not be left to its practitioners.

It is a responsibility of college professors to take counsel with themselves, to assess this problem, and to decide which way the profession should go. If they choose the role of professionalism, then certain behavior patterns are clearly in order, with their chief characteristic being that they will be self-imposed. If they choose to abandon professionalism, then obviously self-imposed restraints are not nearly so necessary, because they will be imposed by society as a whole.

ARE THERE EXTERNAL AND INTERNAL
ROLES OF THE PROFESSOR?

The external role of the college professor can be defined very simply. Under long-standing principles of academic tradition, he is a citizen in every respect and should be accorded the full rights of a citizen when he is performing as one. As a professor, he has certain other obligations which restrict his action. When he is participating in regional or national politics, he should be considered as any other citizen is considered, fully capable of playing a role as a participant in a democracy. Unfortunately, a good many college professors choose to use their status, their title, and their institutional connection as factors in this citizenship role, and this becomes a very unfortunate problem for the entire academic profession. When a professor takes a stand on a political issue and writes a letter to the editor, using his title and his institutional connection, he is abrogating his responsibility as a professional person. The American Association of University Professors fully recognizes this, but the academic profession has not sufficiently policed itself in this matter. A college professor has certain status and prestige—but only as an expert in his special discipline—and if he is willing to use it as leverage in fields outside of his specialty or discipline, he is not performing as a college professor should ethically. In recent years there have been many unfortunate examples of this type of activity by college professors in connection with the military activities of the United States government. Without taking sides on the issues involved, we believe some such incidents have been responsible for the current questioning by government agencies, legislatures, and the public at large, of higher education's ability to manage its own affairs.

In cases such as the above, other college professors should call the offending professor's attention to his actions and remind him of his obligations to the profession. If they do not, and if this becomes a general pattern of behavior as it has in some institutions, then the institution and the entire academic profession are dragged into the role of being protagonists in social and political issues, and the objectivity of scholarship is eroded to the point where academic freedom is threatened.

Internally, the college professor has a tendency to talk in mobile phrases and with great enthusiasm about professional obligations. But, when one of his number is accused of misbehavior by administration or by external forces in society, he has a tendency to close ranks in defense of his colleague, whatever the individual may have done. Society will not long tolerate this type of behavior. College professors must be willing to discipline themselves and their colleagues to keep their own houses in order. They must be fair-minded with regard to offenses committed by other college professors, just as they are with regard to offenses committed by members of society outside the profession. If they demonstrate an unwillingness to be objective with members of their own fraternity, then society may well impose external controls.

WHAT ARE THE RELATIONS OF ACADEME WITH SOCIETY?

Society hopes that higher education will, by passing along to students the conventional wisdom of the past, insure peace and prosperity. The body politic, as well as the Establishment, would have the colleges and universities turn out graduates who, by defending the status quo, would save the world. At the other end of the spectrum is found the liberals who want immediate, sweeping changes in society. They are the anti-Establishment types who create confrontations with non-negotiable demands on the university to change or be destroyed. Somewhere between these two extremes resides the golden mean which, if found and adopted, bids fair to accomplish without apathy or anarchy the goals of both the right and the left. It is the awesome task of educators—especially those on the teaching faculties—to investigate, identify, and illuminate the middle path for all those who would honestly seek the road to wisdom.

History teaches us that this kind of confrontation is not totally new. There have always been extremes and extremists. Perhaps there always will be. And yet, the world has moved forward. This continuous forward movement has been influenced by the great thinkers and teachers of the world. All of them were liberals, progressives, or even radicals in their time. The schools and colleges would, therefore, be untrue to their heritage and responsibility if they did not reflect at least a modicum of the forward-thinking characteristic of those earlier educators.

It is the faculty—the teachers—who must provide the critical and constructive thinking. They can be defended by the boards, supported by the administrators, and succeeded by the students—but, they must provide the leadership through their integrity and intelligence. Indeed, all four segments of the college community, while playing somewhat different roles, are playing on the same stage and in the same production. If each segment—students, faculty, administrators, and trustees—understands its role in the context of the play itself, and plays it properly, then our institutions of higher education will fulfill the great expectations we all hold for them.

Since society creates and sustains these institutions, it has a legitimate right to its expectations. It would be absurd to think that society would encourage those who would destroy it. It is a patient society, in that it will encourage reform. In fact, it expects that its schools, colleges, and universities will innovate, will experiment, will bring about change even in society itself.

It has, therefore, established and supported institutions of higher education for the purpose of providing for (1) *teaching,* or transmitting knowledge; (2) *research,* or developing knowledge; and (3) *service,* or applying knowledge. It has ordained that elected or appointed leaders in the communities will serve as trustees or regents to guide and govern these institutions. They, in turn, select the professional educators who will administer the colleges and universities. The administrators initially select other educators—the faculty—who constitute the corpus of the institutions. It is the faculty that conducts the program—does the teaching, carries on the research, and provides the public service.

While the faculty may be considered the most important, and is certainly the largest, of these three groups, like the other two—members of the board and members of the administration—it exists on campus for educational purposes. Broad as these purposes may be interpreted, they do not include destroying the institutions in order to make what some minorities or militants might consider a better world. Faculties must assume a complex obligation and bear a heavy cross. They must educate with the wisdom of the past, utilizing the most relevant of the present, in order that their students may understand the future. As they educate, not only do they instruct, but they inspire. As they educate, they encourage students to think critically, to analyze, to synthesize, to take and defend positions. As they educate, they must be acutely conscious of the influence they are exerting. It is here that the great ethical question confronts us; to what extent can and should the professor rock the boat, tilt the windmill, or lead the charge?

This is a philosophical question, so we defer to one of the world's great philosophers, a life-long liberal, a gifted teacher, Professor Sidney Hook of New York University: "In the last analysis, it is the faculties who are responsible for the present state of American universities—responsible because of their apathy for what has developed in the past, and for missed educational opportunities. Despite what is said by outsiders, the faculties of most universities possess great powers which they have so far been reluctant to use. No policy in education can succeed without their support. Theirs is the primary responsibility for upholding academic freedom. Now that American higher education is at bay, challenged as it has never been before by forces *within* the academic community, the faculties must marshal the courage to put freedom first, and to defend it accordingly.

"At the same time, as they move to safeguard the integrity of the educational process, faculties should, wherever they are not already doing so, undertake a critical review of all aspects of the curriculum and university life. Provisions should be made for the airings and public discussion of all student grievances. Students should be invited to assess existing courses, methods of teaching, the effectiveness of their teachers, and to make proposals for new courses.

"It is a libel on American educators to imply that they are hostile to educational change. Most past criticism has inveighed against them for making curricular revisions too readily at the first cries of 'relevance' by pressure groups. Educational crackpots, including some head-line hunting administrators, are now rushing to claim that had their curricular panaceas been adopted, student violence would have been avoided. They assiduously ignore the fact that the extremist student groups are trying to bring down bigger game.

"John Dewey was fond of saying that in the modern world there is no such thing as the 'status quo.' Change in education, as in society, is inescapable. The only questions are whether the direction and the content of change are sound, and what the rate and magnitude of change should be. Men of goodwill may differ about the answers. But no matter how profound the differences, they do not justify the resort to violence to impose solutions. In a secular society, the places where human beings assemble to inquire and to reason together should be regarded as sacred ground. Whoever desecrates it, should feel the disapproval of the entire community."[3]

DOCUMENTATION AND COMMENTARY

1. *Webster's New International Dictionary*, Second edition, unabridged, Springfield, Mass.: G. & C. Merriam Company, 1934, 1976.

2. *Bulletin of the American Association of University Professors*, February, 1941, 27:1, 41.

3. Sidney Hook, *The Saturday Review*, April 19, 1969, 55.

BIBLIOGRAPHY

Anderson, Robert H. *Teaching in a World of Change.* New York: Harcourt Brace & World, 1966.

Arrowsmith, William, "The Future of Teaching," keynote address delivered to the American Council on Education, Annual Meeting, October 13, 1966.

Barzun, Jacques. *Teachers in America.* Garden City, New York: Doubleday Anchor Books, 1954.

Berlyne, D. E. *Conflict, Arousal, and Curiosity.* New York: McGraw-Hill Book Company, 1960.

Brown, J. Douglas. *The Liberal University: An Institutional Analysis.* New York: McGraw-Hill Book Company, 1969.

Bulletin of the American Association of University Professors, February, 1941, 27:1, 41, and September, 1967, 53:5, 270-274.

Burns, Gerald P., ed. *Administrators in Higher Education.* New York: Harper and Row, Publishers, 1962.

_____. *Trustees in Higher Education.* New York: Independent College Funds of America, 1966.

Commager, Henry Steele, in *The Saturday Review,* August 17, 1966, 13.

Drucker, Peter F. *Managing for Results.* New York: Harper and Row, Publishers, 1964.

Dunham, E. Alden. *Colleges of the Forgotten Americans.* New York: McGraw-Hill Book Company, 1969.

Educational Record, The, "Teachers and Teaching," Annual Meeting Issue, Summer, 1966, 47:3, 289, 412.

Feldman, Kenneth A., and Theodore M. Newcomb. *The Impact of College on Students.* Vol. I, San Francisco: Jossey-Bass, Inc., 1969.

Hand, Learned. *The Spirit of Liberty.* New York: Vintage Books, 1959.

Henderson, Algo D. *Policies and Practices in Higher Education.* New York: Harper and Brothers, 1960.

Hook, Sidney, in *The Saturday Review,* April 19, 1969, 55.

Horn, Francis, in *U.S. News and World Report,* November 21, 1966, 133.

Ingraham, Mark H., and Francis P. King. *The Outer Fringe—Faculty Benefits Other Than Annuities and Insurance.* Madison, Wisconsin: The University of Wisconsin Press, 1965.

Jencks, Christopher, "An Anti-Academic Proposal," *The Educational Record,* "Teachers and Teaching," Annual Meeting Issue, Summer, 1966, 47:3,321.

——————, and David Riesman. *The Academic Revolution.* Garden City, New York: Doubleday & Company, Inc., 1968.

Ladd, Dwight B. *Change in Educational Policy: Self-Studies in Selected Colleges and Universities.* New York: McGraw-Hill Book Company, 1970.

McGrath, Earl J. *Should Students Share the Power?* Philadelphia: Temple University Press, 1970.

Miller, Richard I. *Evaluating Faculty Performance.* San Francisco: Jossey-Bass, Inc., Publishers, 1972.

Mursell, James L. *Successful Teaching.* New York: McGraw-Hill Company, 1946.

Muscatine, Charles, in *College Management,* May 1967.

Perkins, Dexter, background paper delivered to the American Council on Education, 49th Annual Meeting.

Purks, J. Harris, Jr., Address at the Third State of the University Conference of the University of North Carolina, March 10, 1955.

Ruml, Beardsley, and Donald Morrison. *Memo to a College Trustee.* New York: McGraw-Hill Company, 1959.

Sanford, Nevitt, ed. *The American College.* New York: John Wiley & Sons, Inc., 1962.

Smith, G. Kerry, ed. *The Troubled Campus, Current Issues in Higher Education 1970.* San Francisco: Jossey-Bass, Inc., Publishers, 1970.

Vavoulis, Alexander, "Delegation of Authority, Fact or Myth in University Government," *The Voice of the Faculties,* Association of California State College Professors, October, 1966, 5.

Webster's New International Dictionary. Second edition unabridged. Springfield, Massachusetts: G. & C. Merriam Company, 1934.

INDEX